PRAISE FUK MAKE SPACE TO LEAD

"Refreshing and useful encouragement for reframing our relationship to work."

—**Jake Knapp**, Author of New York Times bestseller *Sprint* and *Make Time*

"If you're stressed out, overworked, and overwhelmed, pick up this book now. It'll inspire you to start running actionable experiments to make more space in your life."

—**Dorie Clark**, Author of *The Long Game*
and Executive Education Faculty, Duke University Fuqua School of Business

"This book is a welcome addition to the libraries of leaders at all levels! As a leader who is often guilty of "worship at the cult of busy," I found myself in many aspects of this book. This relatable read is full of actionable tools— for succeeding at work, and in all parts of life. Through Tutti's personal experiences of leadership and her clients' stories, she gives us permission to deeply reflect, and slow down, to achieve even greater success."

—**Catherine Courage**, VP Consumer UX at Google and Author of
Understanding Your Users: A Practical Guide to User Research Methods

"Watching Tutti's personal transformation as she makes space for the meaningful values in her life has been incredibly inspiring. In this book, she lays out the frameworks and tools that will help you achieve the change you're looking for."

—**Julie Zhuo**, New York Times bestselling Author of
The Making of a Manager and former VP Design at Facebook

"Tutti Taygerly integrates her love of surfing and design to inspire us towards transformation. Read this book now for insights and tools to teach us that slowing down is the path towards a successful career."

—**Maria Giudice**, Author of *Rise of the DEO: Leadership by Design*

"Tutti Taygerly delves deeply into the 'cult of busyness' and what happens when we step out of that rush to find what we really want. Through her stories and coaching insight, we gather the advice we need to step into the unknown, bravely experiment, and find ourselves."

—**Alana Karen**, Author of *The Adventures of Women in Tech:
How We Got Here and Why We Stay* and Director at Google

"*Make Space to Lead* challenges the idea that grind it out at all costs is the one path to success. Tutti shares her personal path to leadership as well the journeys from her clients in Silicon Valley where success often comes at cost. Whether you are go-go-go or wondering if there is a better way to achieve success than hustle and burnout, pause, take a deep breath, and make space to read this book."

—**Donna Lichaw**, Executive Coach and Author of *The User's Journey -
Storymapping Products That People Love*

"If you have drunk the tech industry kool-aid that you need to always be hustling and found it to be toxic, *Make Space To Lead* is the perfect antidote.

In *Make Space To Lead*, Tutti Taygerly openly, generously and honestly shares her personal journey into making space in her life to make her a better leader and coach."

—**Andy Polaine**, Design Leadership Coach and Co-Author of
Service Design: From Insight to Implementation.

"We live in a world where doing is more important than being. Tutti Taygerly's life-changing book helps you break the patterns of joyless busyness. Her personal stories, thought experiments, and practical strategies show you how to create space to not only live a life of purpose but do so with deep satisfaction and joy. Buy this book!"

— **Leonard Szymczak**, Psychotherapist and bestselling Author
of *The Roadmap Home: Your GPS to Inner Peace* and
award-winning Author of *Kookaburra's Last Laugh*

"*Make Space to Lead* is a must-read for high-achievers who are (finally) seeking full-spectrum success."

— **David Taylor-Klaus**, Coach, Speaker, and Author of *Mindset Mondays with DTK: 52 Ways to REWIRE Your Thinking and Transform Your Life*

MAKE

SPACE

TO

LEAD

Taygerly Labs Inc

San Francisco, CA

www.tuttitaygerly.com

This book is designed to provide information and motivation to our readers. The opinions expressed in the book are solely that of its author and of no employer that the author has worked for. No warranties or guarantees are expressed or implied by the publisher's choice to include any of the content in this book. The publisher is not engaged to render any type of professional advice or services to the individual reader. The discussion or mention of any ideas, frameworks, inquiries, products, and suggestions in this book is not intended as a substitute for consulting with your physician, therapist, or other qualified professional. Neither the author or the publisher shall be liable for any physical, psychological, emotional, financial, or commercial damages. Our views and rights are the same: You are responsible for your own choices, actions, and outcomes.

While the examples and case studies in this book are drawn from real client engagements, the names and identifying details of persons mentioned have been changed or omitted to protect their privacy.

ISBN: 978-1-7379983-2-7 — hardcover

ISBN: 978-1-7379983-1-0 — paperback

ISBN: 978-1-7379983-0-3 — e-book

Library of Congress Control Number: 2021919621

Cover and interior design: Dino Marino

MAKE

SPACE

TO

LEAD

BREAK PATTERNS TO FIND FLOW AND FOCUS ON WHAT MATTERS

TUTTI TAYGERLY

EXPERIMENT WORKBOOK

To continue the conversation, download your free copy of the *Make Space to Lead* Experiment Workbook. It includes all the experiments from this book in an easy-to-print format so you can start running your own experiments.

Download it for free at

tuttitaygerly.com/makespaceexperiment

TABLE OF CONTENTS

INTRODUCTION

The me from five years ago, the Tutti of 2016, would not recognize the me of today. I don't think that we would be friends. I was a woman consumed by an inner achievement monster that drove me to keep doing more. I was an intense control freak focused on perfection. Yes, there are some traits and values that are consistent for the both of us. I was, and am, a fiercely driven, ambitious woman. I valued adventure and risk. The difference is that now I'm like that surfer waiting for the next big wave—both content and primed for action.

Five years ago, I was one-hundred-percent a designer who solved problems and got shit done—a Do-er. On the spectrum of Being versus Doing, the world we live in values the Doing. We stay continually active, moving through life, keeping busy, and looking for the next problem to solve. At work, we run down our to-do lists, completing task after task and only briefly pausing in the satisfaction of earning our gold stars for the day. At home, we run through the familiar pattern of meal prep, chores, commuting, and perhaps a little bit of relaxation with some shows or games, before getting ready for bed and preparing to repeat the pattern tomorrow.

Yet, so rarely do we stop and take time to *Be* and to acknowledge our value. Making space is the *Being* part of our lives, the blank space between checking off all the items on the to-do list. Making space is giving ourselves permission to slow down and savor each moment of our life, because it's valuable and we are valuable. As high achievers, we need to integrate both our value as a Human Be-ing and a Human Do-er.

For decades, I'd felt this nagging energy that told me that I needed to work harder and do more to prove myself to the world. I listened to the voice of an inner achievement monster that told me how to achieve professional and personal success. I thought I had learned the system for success after becoming high school Valedictorian, getting a Human-Computer Interaction degree from Stanford University, and then rising up the corporate ladder to become a world-class design leader at Facebook. I thought it was about marrying my college sweetheart, having two wonderful daughters, buying a house in San Francisco, and spending our leisure time vacationing in fabulous international destinations. These were the things I was supposed to do, right?

Wrong.

I was a zombie, stuck on autopilot, living someone else's dreams and values. Professionally, I used design thinking to solve problems for the companies I worked for. I used the design process that had divergence— opening to multiple solutions using tools such as brainstorming—and convergence—narrowing to a small set of choices to move forward and experiment with. Yet I spent very little time introspecting and questioning the patterns I was stuck in. I had zero space in my life to figure out what truly mattered to me.

Have you continually kept on running, using busyness as a badge of honor, and looking for the next shiny project, company, person to spend your energy on? Because if you stopped, life would feel empty.

Have you struggled with being a workaholic? Because it's easier to pour time and attention into getting gold stars from a set of clear corporate standards, rather than figure out how to deal with the complexity of coworkers, friends or family members.

Me too. All these struggles and worries kept me up at night, when my subconscious mind was finally allowed the space to wander and think about what mattered. Yet, come daylight, the push for efficiency and achievement pushed all these thoughts to the side. I had too many important things to do.

The me of five years ago was working as a design leader at Facebook. Many people think that working for Facebook would be a dream job. Sure, at first, it was my dream job. I had followed the traditional path of success through twenty-two years of design jobs in start-ups, design agencies, and large companies. For over two decades, I had worked fifty to seventy hours a week in corporations, serving other people's goals. At Facebook, I built completely new video products that showcased diverse voices and new forms of interactivity. Each day I felt exhilarated. And at the same time, I was bone-tired, overwhelmed, and anxious. I was constantly Do-ing: running at one-hundred-and-ten percent, jumping from crucial meeting to crucial meeting, always multi-tasking, and being 'on'. I was constantly running out of time. These challenges were compounded by my three-hour daily commute. No matter how hard I painstakingly prioritized, it was impossible to get everything done. I couldn't do enough, and I never paused just to *be*. I was giving up the best hours of my days, and maybe the best years of my life, in service to someone else's vision and purpose.

Something had to change. So, I quit.

I left the security and prestige of Facebook. The company makes it hard to leave: You are surrounded by ridiculously smart people, making products that impact 2.3 billion people globally, while cocooned in an idyllic place where growth and learning are emphasized. Also, the food is delicious (seriously). When your work with one team is ending, you are encouraged to transfer to another team within the broad world of Facebook, Instagram, WhatsApp, or Oculus. When I left the Video team after three years, I couldn't find the passion I needed to join another team, to be truly inspired to lead a team of product designers. So, I left Facebook.

I had been coaching teams of designers for ten-plus years. Facebook gave me the training and skills to coach female technologists throughout the company. I'd worked with my own executive coaches for the past eight years, and they helped me find my own unique leadership while integrating parts of the feedback I received.

After I left Facebook, I took my first coaching workshops through the Co-active Training Institute. I figured that it would help me be a better leader—a better listener who could influence others. I figured that it would help me in my next design leadership job. That wasn't the message that the universe had for me, though. Even though something in me fought it—kicking and screaming—I decided to take a big career experiment and struck out on my own. I started with a foundation of leadership coaching and have now expanded to consulting, teaching, running retreats, and writing.

My surfing journey has paralleled this career growth. I learned to surf in my late twenties. I poured my driven, ambitious personality into scrambling and jockeying to surf the best waves. When I moved to San Francisco in my early thirties, I wanted to paddle out at the fiercest, biggest breaks and Ocean Beach is notorious for being the most challenging. It was a badge of honor to battle your way past the endless, cold waves, duck-diving for forty-five minutes to make it out to the lineup at Ocean Beach. I needed to hit my goals—wake up early to make it to the beach, paddle out to the lineup, and catch three waves down the line. Despite all that Do-ing, over the years the ocean gave me space. It shaped me to become a different person. I learned that I didn't always have to brute-force my way through the waves; instead, I could bask in the flow and peace surfing brought me. That flow is the beauty of floating out on the ocean, surrounded by the ever-shifting ecosystem. That flow is the rhythm of waves as I sit encircled by sea life. Above my head, pelicans and birds swoop through the water looking for fish. One day, I'm delighted to be sharing the waves with three dolphins, arching their way down the line. Another spring day, I see whales breaching in the distance. One rare time, I catch a glimpse of a baby otter floating on its back, as it cracked open an urchin to reach its delicious center. Not to mention, the mystery of wondering how many great white sharks were silently sweeping through the depths beneath. Surfing is my space for quiet rejuvenation. I yearned for this kind of space in my professional life, too, but I couldn't find it until I left Facebook.

I wrote this book to share what I've learned. I share tools that I've used to support countless high achievers in and out of Silicon Valley through their own leadership journeys. I coached my clients using the design process—opening up to different perspectives and focusing on the next choice. We established North Stars for the life they wanted to create. We broke patterns that were now limiting, and most importantly, we created small experiments to try out different actions in the process of becoming better leaders.

I wrote this book because I've finally learned to embrace a surfing approach to work and life (I share this S.U.R.F model in Chapter Eight).

I've slowed down and integrated the Being as well as the Doing. I've practiced the tools and inner resources to not need as much certainty and control over the impossible chaos of life. This skill proved invaluable as I built a new business for myself and learned to lead my own company.

While the details of what I do each year will change, I'm no longer searching for elusive external success. I am content and fulfilled with the work I do, its impact on the world, and the relationships and connections I have with the people I care about. I actually like myself and the leader I am right now. She's a person I want to be friends with. I've learned that space matters, and I will continue to make space to lead.

CHAPTER ONE

OVERWHELMED BY BUSYNESS

For most of my life, I've worshipped at the altar of busyness.

In high school, I packed my schedule with everything I possibly could. I attended an elite school in New Delhi, India. Our fathers were diplomats, leaders of international businesses, and wealthy Indians. My father ran the ground operations for Thai Airways and wasn't around a lot. As Station Manager, he worked nights, because the flights from Europe to Thailand would pass through New Delhi in the early hours of the morning. My "tiger mom" was around all the time and would lavish me with love and approval when I did well in school and when I filled my days with useful activities. With my American classmates, I took every possible Advanced Placement (AP) class, but those were looked down upon as "easy" by my classmates. The more ambitious program was the International Baccalaureate (IB) program, universally viewed as more rigorous than AP and was meant to be the world-class standard for secondary education. My classmates from the rest of the world enrolled in the IB program, so I did, too. To fulfill the requirements, I had to excel at the traditional academic subjects, be fluent in multiple languages, develop my ability to think critically in a theory of knowledge class, and fulfill hours of community service to learn empathy and demonstrate kindness to those around us. My days were packed with classes, homework, volunteering in the slums of New Delhi, and endless practice for the rounds of oral exams needed to demonstrate proficiency at IB. At night, I would sneak out of the house to party with my classmates everywhere we could—at the hotel clubs and bars, and even amongst the parks and historic ruins of an ancient city. I was fifteen. I didn't need a lot of sleep. My rebel side needed a release valve from the continual pressures of high school.

I entered Stanford University when I was sixteen; after graduating in 1997, I started working as a designer in Silicon Valley. I reveled in being "busy" with my weekly and monthly milestones at work. I felt proud, like I was an important contributor to the tech companies and their impactful work. Throughout my twenty-two-year career in start-ups, design firms, and large technology companies, including my last corporate job at Facebook, I held up my busyness like a badge of honor. After all, that's what had been engrained in me since I was a little girl. I'd never thought to question it.

Whenever anyone said: "Hey, how are you?" I had a standard answer.

With pride, I would let out an audible sigh and reply, "Phew, so crazy busy. You?"

One moment, when I'd just started my new job at Facebook in 2015, stands out: A good friend from college, who I hadn't seen in several years, was in town and asked if she could stop by for lunch the next day. I paused in astonishment at her audacity before I snippily ran her through my packed meeting schedule. I told her (with pride) that I was already double-booked for lunch. I followed that with an indifferent half-shrug and said, "You really need to let me know at least a week ahead." That opportunity for spontaneous connection and cherished space with a dear friend evaporated in the face of my busyness. It would be another six months before she and I spent time together face-to-face. Back at my laptop, I felt a brief twinge of regret before blithely pushing the interaction out of my awareness. I leaned into my packed schedule even more deeply.

Every day, I ran from meeting to meeting. For lunch, I'd grab nuts or a bar from the well-stocked snack bins provided by tech companies. If I was lucky, I'd conduct a lunch interview, which combined my need for fuel with the company's need to recruit designers. Several years later, once I made the space to provide emotional safety to my teams, people shared that when they stopped by my desk to chat, my frosty glare and aloof body language indicated to them that I needed to get back to the urgent emails and pings on my laptop. I felt important, but I had made them feel small and unimportant, as though they were bothering me and not worthy of my attention. I felt the shame of a self-absorbed leader; I'd unintentionally devalued the people I most wanted to support and serve.

Every workday, I rushed endlessly from conference room to conference room, rapidly context-switching on the fly. In meetings, I would sometimes multitask instead of paying attention to the people in front of me, in the hopes that I could instead clear out some "urgent" emails. Often it felt like these meetings were just busywork, stealing away valuable time that I could have used to do myriad other tasks. Despite my feelings, I couldn't stop attending the meetings—it felt like a status symbol to have that seat at the table. I often felt that I was simply treading water to get through the day. My creative work—writing strategy documents or crafting presentations—was shunted to evenings when no one would disturb me.

I packed my weekends with grocery shopping, cooking in bulk for the week, planning for summer camps and vacations, running the kids around to their playdates, soccer games and practices, plus making sure I exercised and had some adult time with friends.

Having a packed calendar and a long to-do list both for my job and the work of home helped give me structure to get things done. I didn't stop to deeply prioritize how I spent my time. It *all* felt important. I couldn't afford to ditch or say no to any part of it, or so I believed. I was afraid of missing out on something important. Every day was structured into neat thirty-minute intervals, so I could believe I was always doing something of value.

I'd learned my lesson well as a high-achieving student and daughter: Being productive is better than being lazy. I received the love and approval I needed only when I kept my head down and did all the things that my parents and teachers wanted me to do. *Doing* things meant that I was of value, that I had value. When my days were overflowing with tasks to do and people to see, I believed that meant that I was skilled and important. People wanted me to do things for them! People wanted to meet with me! I kept reacting, without question, to other people who told me what was important.

I had been taught that achieving tasks and ticking them off my list was a measure of my performance and my innate worth. This message resonates with a lot of my clients, and I expect that since you're reading this book, it may also resonate with you. Through experience, I learned that if I paused to take a breath or—god forbid—to rest, then I would feel immense shame and anxiety about my laziness. I racked up gold stars of achievement by checking items off my to-do list and completing each rectangle appointment in my calendar. To allow empty space would have meant that I had nothing to do—unacceptable. I was afraid that if I did nothing, other people would judge me as being unproductive and unworthy of my seat at the table. I needed to fill, if not double or triple-fill all the whitespace—in design, the negative space between the content—in my weekdays and weekends. This addiction to constant doing is happening to us all. Perhaps it's sustainable for a brief period of days, weeks, or even years to get through an intense period, however, it's impossible to maintain this pace for the long-term. I've learned to pause, slow down, and look beyond the busyness to connect with how I wanted to sustainably live and work.

THE POWER OF WORDS

I remember when I received media training at Facebook, before I was to speak at the South by Southwest (SxSW) music and technology conference. The trainer told me that those of us in tech tend to speak in Silicon Valley jargon; we assume that everyone speaks our language and shares our common frame of understanding. In particular, the trainer called out my usage of the term "dogfooding."

In tech companies, the term "dogfooding" gets used often. *Dogfooding* means testing your product internally—eating your own dogfood—to experience what it feels like before launching publicly. A company's employees use the product to help work out many of the biggest kinks and flaws of a product before it is released to a broader audience.

"Words create worlds."[1] This saying is attributed to Rabbi Abraham Joseph Heschel, Jewish philosopher and a leader in the civil rights movement. We use jargon as shorthand for the purpose of efficiency. We also use jargon as a secret code to share with those in the know, to implicitly establish a sense of belonging, a special language that only us insiders can wield. The media trainer emphasized that in this particular context (SxSW), using a piece of tech vernacular when the audience was mostly journalists and general attendees, would reinforce the impression that Silicon Valley—and especially Facebook—is elitist and out of touch

Words can reframe
our reality, helping
us to connect with
or repel others.

with the regular world. This wasn't the kind of impact I wanted to have; instead, I yearned to connect and teach others. I learned that I needed to be careful with my words. Words can reframe our reality, helping us to connect with or repel others.

DOGFOODING AT FACEBOOK

Rather than relying on the standard Google or Microsoft calendars that many companies use, Facebook believed in building tools and software for internal use. The company built a proprietary internal calendar tool, and every employee used this to keep control of our busyness and our days.

We dogfooded new features for the product. One day, a mysterious little number appeared on the top of our calendar tool. This innocuous number showed the total amount of hours that you were in meetings. It prompted a flurry of conversation and messages among my colleagues. Our reactions were mixed. Some designers laughed and thought this was a silly exercise—they were happy with their low number. Ambitious others wanted to see how high their number was compared with the packed schedules of their managers. I stared at my tiny little number, almost hidden amongst the omnipresent color-coding and crowded rectangles stacked on the screen, and worried that it was too low, that I wasn't busy enough. My first instinct was to see how I compared with other leaders.

With a delighted sigh of relief, I saw that mine was amongst the highest of the numbers. This was validation. I WAS important. I sat with that feeling for some minutes or hours, or it could have been days of egotistical pride.

However, over the coming weeks, I couldn't stop thinking about that number. It didn't seem like having such a high number meant that I was winning. I wasn't sure that I enjoyed being in meetings all the time. I loved my job, or so I thought. I loved reviewing designs and making sure that they solved specific needs for Facebook users. I loved collaborating with peers from other departments or platforms to come up with the best solutions. I loved presenting long-term strategy to our leadership team and persuading them that *this* vision would truly improve Facebook users' lives.

Yet that meeting hours number stayed with me. It triggered a kernel of discontent. It made me feel ashamed, but I didn't know why. I was starting to become defined by that number. I was drinking the Kool-Aid of Facebook's mission to connect the world and it made me feel smug about my number. Yet at the same time, the same meetings and work that I thought I loved weren't making me feel great. I felt stressed, overwhelmed, invariably behind, and I constantly believed I would never catch up.

As I worked my long hours, I ignored my friends and husband, spent less time with my two little girls, and overcompensated with lavish gifts and jam-packed weekends to make the most of our brief time together. Each day was a nightmarish exercise of ruthless, endless prioritization. I felt a mixture of pride that I was helping everyone else with their important things and also resentment, because I wasn't sure how much I believed in their importance. Whether this was intentional or not, the dogfooding brought to light how many hours I spent in meetings, and the extent to which I was defining my worth against this clarifying number. That was the first time I realized how much I was buying into the cult of busyness, and I was beginning to experience how truly addictive and soul-crushing it was.

I wish I could say that I took immediate action and started planning a different, more fulfilling life. I could have used this awareness to start dreaming of something different. I might have had conversations with others about this kernel of discontent. But for the most part, I put my head down and kept working. I continued my daily worship at the altar of busy. This happens to all of us. Change starts with a little kernel of insight. It sits at the back of our mind and can take weeks, months, or even years of pondering before we're ready to act on it.

Each day as I opened my laptop, I saw that number in my calendar. I couldn't shake the feeling that something was wrong. Once that took root, my inner voice of knowing kept questioning the value of that number. I needed to create more space, both for myself and for everyone around me who bought into the value of a high number. We discussed it in team meetings, and I asked my team to keep me accountable to lowering my number each week. I talked to my peers who led teams and started to bring it up in conversation to see how they felt about the number. Increasingly,

Change starts with a little kernel of insight. It sits at the back of our mind and can take weeks, months, or even years of pondering before we're ready to act on it.

I was developing more resonance and understanding with others who were also questioning the benefits of constant busyness.

Slowly over the months and years that followed, I obsessively dreamed about making more space in my life. I got curious. *What would happen if I slowed down?* I wondered. *Would I lose my edge? Was I the only person who felt this way? Was this even normal?*

CLIENT STORY:
THE PUSH TO WORK LONGER HOURS

One of my clients, Soraya, is a bright, driven female engineer working at a start-up developing cutting edge technology. When I met her, she was in her first "player-coach" role—a phrase taken from baseball—where some assistant coaches are also players. Soraya did some hands-on work, and she simultaneously strategized, planned, and directed the work of others. When she came to me, she was confused. She was finally being recognized for her hard work, yet the increasing pressure was destroying her confidence. At the end of each workday, she confessed to crying for long periods, freaking out because there was so much to do and not enough time. She wanted help mastering her own emotions and stress so that she could be even more productive.

In one of our sessions, Soraya was especially distraught. The previous two weeks had been particularly grueling. The company's most important project was two months behind schedule and she had just been handed the lead role for the project. Her manager expected Soraya to turn it around and get it completed to meet the client's deadlines in three weeks. She was at her wits end. She was working all the time, and yet couldn't get enough done.

I said, "Tell me about your working hours."

Soraya's typical schedule was to wake up at 6am, formally start work at 8am, and wrap up work around 8pm to have dinner with her family. However, she would get pinged almost every day with urgent tasks by both the US and Asia division teams from 7am to 10pm. She typically worked most of the day on Saturdays, but she was proud of holding the line to not work on Sundays.

I asked her, "How is this schedule working for you?"

Soraya shared that she wasn't sleeping; she was making a lot of "silly little mistakes;" and she often ended up crying with frustration, anxiety, and disappointment. She'd gotten to a point where, as she said, "my mind doesn't want to work as it's constantly tired." She craved more time with her family, her cat, and even with herself so she could replenish her energy. "I want to be able to do nothing and sit in silence," she told me.

It's always easier to see contradictions and misalignment in other people than it is to see it in ourselves. Soraya yearned to be a successful leader, to be the person who would support her company by rescuing this key project. She would be central to the company's success in this crucial early stage. Yet she only had one mode of working—to push herself to work harder and longer hours. She was driving herself to exhaustion and burnout. This wasn't sustainable.

Soraya had been working beyond her maximum capacity for months. She was burned out, completely depleted mentally, physically, and emotionally. She was at her wits end and worried that she might rage-quit a job that she loved, simply to make the overwhelm go away. She had nothing else to lose.

Soraya was ready to experiment and try something a little different. She didn't quite believe that making space and working fewer hours would help how she felt, but her back was up against the wall. She initiated some conversations with her boss about her burnout. He was sincerely and fully supportive of Soraya finding ways to give herself a break. She was receiving feedback along the same lines: managers and peers had been telling her for months that in order to grow as a leader, she needed to learn how to delegate more and do less hands-on work herself.

With this context and self-understanding, Soraya and I co-created some experiments for her to both cut down the number of hours she was working as well as to maximize her focus time during her work hours. We settled on two experiments:

1. **Establish boundaries around her work, to limit how "on-call" she would be to answer urgent pings.** She would only be available 7am–7pm Monday to Friday, and 9am–11am on Saturdays. We brainstormed personal activities that would nourish her and she could spend her weekday mornings and evenings on those activities, instead of working.

2. **Invest time in solving the true problem.** She was in a short-term bind because the team was understaffed, and she had multiple people to hire. The time she spent doing her immediate company tasks was time spent away from ultimately fixing the long-term desire to lead as a creative problem-solver. She was able to make space to grow other leaders on the team by teaching and delegating. She was also able to prioritize spending more time on hiring and recruiting.

Neither of these experiments was a magic bullet. Some of the activities worked, and others didn't. Sometimes the hours-boundary held and sometimes it didn't. However, taking the time to recognize that she was stuck in the cult of busy, and her understanding that it was unwinnable and emotionally impossible, gave Soraya some perspective to try new ways to move forward. She was still busy and worked on many immediate projects, however, she had more energy when she made space for her own activities and returned to work better rested. She grew as a leader as she made room for others to lead.

It was only a tiny bit of breathing room, yet Soraya was able to make some space to protect herself from burnout. She recognized that the company had many months and years of shipping products ahead, and she had to pace herself for the long run. She started to make space for family, video games, kickboxing, and journaling—all activities that sustained her and built up her mental, emotional, and physical reserves.

When we're on the edge of burnout, there's often too much going on for us to recognize what a precarious situation it is.

When we're on the edge of burnout, there's often too much going on for us to recognize what a precarious situation it is. The first step is to become aware that there is a problem and that something needs to give. Once you can take that pause—often the biggest step—then it opens up space for experiments to try to address the busyness. For many of my clients, the steps are similar to Soraya's—first establish some boundaries to claim your time (quick win). Then, with that tiny bit of extra space, invest effort in solving the longer-term problem. For example, spending more time on recruiting or delegating and training up others.

FOCUS BLOCKS AT FACEBOOK

As my time continued at Facebook, I grew increasingly aware of the need for time and space, especially for designers responsible for dreaming up new products and features. To affect change at a tech company like Facebook, you needed to show hard data to justify a shift. This data-driven method is how I lived my life while working in technology. I'm a skeptic and I need to see the explanation or rationalization before I'm willing to run an experiment.

Facebook sent out surveys to every employee twice a year. These were known as Pulse surveys and the intent was to better understand how employees felt about the company, the organization, their manager, and their own level of satisfaction with work. The company, organization, and manager Pulse metrics could be tracked over years to see trends around employee satisfaction and optimism, and these were mapped against how the company was perceived in the media. As design team leaders, we noticed a disturbing trend among the team: Designers were growing less satisfied with their work. Specifically, the answers to a question— "How often do you have the opportunities to do what you do best?" were disproportionately lower compared to other disciplines such as engineering or product management. As we dug deeper into diagnosing the problem, we learned that designers felt increasingly required to respond to urgent inbound requests from other teams. They didn't feel like they had the space or time to do long-term thinking, visionary work, or planning beyond the immediate daily, weekly, or monthly tasks that had to be accomplished. This was a complex problem that the leadership team was eager to solve; we wanted to try to make designers' lives better.

One of the issues with being overwhelmed, with having too much to do, is that we believe the sole solution is multitasking. We are conditioned to believe that we can be more efficient when performing multiple tasks at once, and are certain that technology can help us with this. We can be in a meeting while simultaneously clearing out our inbox and responding to urgent messages. Neuroscience research[2] has shown that our brain isn't actually capable of performing multiple tasks at the same time. Multitasking is a myth. The reality is that we rapidly switch from task to task with such haste that our conscious minds think we're doing them simultaneously. Our brain quickly stops and starts new tasks, as we switch contexts and activities endlessly. In fact, the most efficient approach is to focus on a single task.

I'm one-hundred-percent guilty of multitasking. I'm also guilty of complacently thinking about the *other* research, which says that even though multitasking doesn't really work, women are better able to multitask than men[3]. I have used that research to justify my attempts to answer my daughter's urgent question about locating her soccer cleats while simultaneously attempting to coach a client over Zoom. Yet deep down, I know that I'm trying to shove more tasks into a limited amount of time.

I think of my Chrome browser window and how it often has thirty-plus tabs open, an indication of all the things I'm juggling and trying to pay attention to in my busyness. I remember one day, I went to my company's IT department, nicknamed Helpdesk, and complained about my laptop's slow performance. The Helpdesk man laughed, then he pointed out the number of tabs I had open. "If you start closing the tabs you don't need," he said, "everything will work faster." I walked out of the Helpdesk, a little irritated that he didn't have a tech fix to my problem, yet also sheepish that the solution was a simple one that I was resisting. It just didn't seem right that the answer to being overwhelmed was as simple as shutting down all the excess information bungling around both my brain and the browser.

After multiple rounds of conversations and experiments with different leaders at Facebook, we eventually decided to experiment with closing all the thirty-plus unneeded tabs in our mental browser windows, at least for a set period of time. We called these focus blocks.

Focus blocks are long periods of time when employees were freed from the tyranny of meetings and other people's agendas, so they could get some of their own work done. Ideally, this allocated time was three to four hours long, multiple times a week. Each person could schedule the time on the calendar to support the individual rhythms of their best work times. The beauty behind this approach is that people get an uninterrupted block (section of time) to focus on larger projects, without the distractions of meetings or pressures from multitasking. For designers at Facebook, this allocated space in their calendar allowed them to fiercely protect their "maker" time. They received freedom from thirty-minute chunks of sliced-up calendars to allow them the luxury of diving deep into the work that they did best. Focus blocks are a handy calendar structure to encourage a state of flow and the energy that comes with the gift of time.

Focus blocks weren't a new idea. The concept had been discussed and tried in many technology companies that struggled with the same scarcity of time as Facebook. These set aside time periods worked well for some designers at Facebook. It worked even better when we could get entire teams of people–designers, engineers, and product managers–to all commit to one or two set periods of time in a week when everyone could benefit from a deep dive into their most cherished work. This was in addition to the practice of "no meeting Wednesdays" to allow similar periods away from the busyness of a packed schedule.

It wasn't a panacea. Yet it was one small step, an initial experiment to play with freedom from overwhelm. It may seem counterintuitive—how could I possibly have the spare time to block out three-four hours when I'm so busy?—yet I've found it invaluable for my clients. I personally take day-long focus blocks every month to map out a long view of my business. Both my weekly focus blocks on Mondays and the hours I spend surfing are where some of my best ideas emerge.

EXPERIMENT:
TRY USING FOCUS BLOCKS

- Take a look at your calendar. What weekdays are the most free? Which days and times do you have the most energy? When are you most alive to do this focused work? If you do it after a brutal day, you'll not be very efficient. I do it first thing in the morning—bonus points if it's post-surf—because that is when I am most creative. Play around with times to see what works for you.

- Pick a day to block out a three-four hour chunk of time. You might need to look several weeks out. You might need to cancel or move some meetings.

- Block out the time in your calendar. Name it something inspiring or fun such as Creative Visioning, My Time to Dream, or DO NOT F*CKING DISTURB.

- Try it once. See how it feels. Consider making it a regular part of your week or month.

MAKING SPACE FOR WHAT MATTERS

I was raised by an Asian "tiger mom" who believed in education and rote memorization. She also believed that long hours and hard effort were the keys to success. She had put my older sister through many years of enforced piano lessons, which I'd mercifully avoided because it was too difficult to keep hauling a piano around as we moved between multiple countries. Nevertheless, she made sure that every hour of my day was filled.

After decades of hard-earned experience, what I've come to see when working with my clients is that how we spend our time is the reflection of what we choose to value and prioritize. I kept adding more to my plate and doing more. This constant doing made me an overwhelmed, stressed multitasker, perpetually on the edge of burnout. I could see this life reflected in my daughters' schedules. I'd gone back to work when my eldest daughter was just six weeks old—during the recession of 2008—because that's what the design firm I worked for expected. I got a little wiser with my second daughter and took three months of maternity leave before I went back to work. For all my daughters' lives, they'd adjusted to a schedule of being in daycare, preschool, school plus aftercare from 8am through 6pm each day. I had grown up conditioned in the Cult of Busy and continued this pattern through most of my adult life. I was conditioning my children the same way.

But. But. But. I didn't want them to be like me.

The way out of this overwhelm, for me and for you, is to find and make space for what really matters. Soraya learned that she could start experimenting with cutting her hours and saying no. At Facebook, we learned that the tasks and work are endless. What mattered wasn't becoming more efficient, but rather, to be able to do our best work. In order to do that, we had to slow down and have focus blocks. We all need to learn how to pause, take a breath and start to see a way out of this overwhelm. Surfing made me realize that I had the ability to pause and drift with the waves and still fiercely paddle for the next wave I wanted to ride. If I missed it, there's always another wave.

RESEARCH INQUIRY:
UNDERSTAND THE PROBLEM

The first step of the design process is awareness and definition of the problem. To do that, we start with research. If you resonate to these feelings of overwhelm and continual busyness, start by asking yourself the following questions. Try to approach them with a sense of curiosity and without judgement. It can be helpful to write the answers in a journal or reflect on the questions when you're more relaxed, perhaps when taking a walk outside in nature.

- Which days of the week do you feel the most anxiety? What's happening on those days? Which days feel calmer and are infused with higher levels of energy?

  - Notice if there's a difference between the start of the week and the end of the week. Or weekdays versus weekends. Many people have a Sunday night sense of dread before starting the work week. Others feel energized mid-week.

- What activities give you energy? What do you do that brings you joy? What are you grateful for? When are you at your best?

  - Focus on what you need to do, not what you don't want to do.

  - For some people, it's the heads-down maker time and for others it's collaboration sessions with certain people.

- What activities suck your energy?

  - Notice if there's people, tasks or processes that absolutely drain you

- What parts of your life are you neglecting? If you had an extra four hours a week, what would you do with it?

  - You give time and attention to the most urgent fire in front of you, and that's often with work. Consider what else you passively ignore in favor of work.

- How long have you been overwhelmed by busyness?

Many of my clients will jump into weeks or even a month of intense work time when it's absolutely needed. Then they'll go back to a more stable state of normalcy that works for them. Consider if this busyness is temporary or chronic. It makes a difference if you feel like you've been in this state for weeks, months, or years.

These research questions are thought-starters to help you explore and figure out what's going on. You might be ready to move into action and try an experiment, like Soraya's exercise with setting boundaries at work or the Facebook concept of focus blocks. Perhaps it could be a simple experiment like talking to a friend about it. But first, simply take the time to do this research inquiry to better understand what you need to move beyond the busyness.

CHAPTER TWO

THE FEAR OF NOT ACHIEVING

As a designer, I have been addicted to the pursuit of perfection. I wanted every single creative endeavor to be pixel perfect and finely crafted with zero mistakes. I pushed myself constantly to do more and achieve the next highest standard. I was afraid that other people would judge me, that my efforts weren't good enough. And when they didn't judge me, I judged myself, fearing that I would never achieve enough. It's an impossibly high bar, built on unrealistic expectations and inhuman standards.

As the child of an exacting mother whose love was dependent on meeting her high expectations, I grew up striving for perfection, yet I continually felt like I missed the mark. My inner achievement monster had an endless appetite that could only be fed by doing more, making it better, and eliminating all the possible faults.

Today, a quote on a tiny tray on my desk declares: "*Perfection is boring.*" It reminds me that it's impossible to be flawless, that being imperfect, making mistakes, being wild are all part of the joy of being human. It's unreasonable to expect an existence without challenges. And even if it were possible, how boring would it be to live a picture-perfect life? Embracing mess, emotions, and even our fears of not achieving, is all part of what makes us interesting. It defines our authentic leadership. For many decades of my life, this standard for myself, together with big ambition, brought me all the trappings of external success. That made my parents proud. In those same decades, this addiction to achievement became an all-consuming drive, pushing me to achieve what society viewed as success.

FEEDING THE ACHIEVEMENT MONSTER

I was conditioned to be a perfect achiever as a little girl. My mother didn't have a professional job outside the home. She'd given up her career when my older sister was born. From all accounts, she had been wickedly smart at her private boarding school in Hong Kong. She earned a coveted Madame Chang Kai Shek scholarship to attend university at Wellesley. When her family lacked the funds to cover transport to the United States, she arranged multiple endowments and logistical support to get herself there by boat, halfway across the world. She forged her way alone, separated from everyone she knew. She had this "tiger" fierceness that was a model for my drive. It was the only way she knew how to express love. My achievement monster was born from needing to do well at school. To do exactly as I was told. To be quiet and polite. Then I would have achieved status as the perfect little girl who came from a perfect mother.

My mother often yelled at me for my mistakes. I tried hard at school and did well. I was always at the top of my class. I loved collecting shiny gold stars from my teachers. But it wasn't enough. I got an A- in one of my classes. That little minus marred the perfect record of expected As and A+s. I was afraid to bring that grade home because I already knew that I was a disappointment. "Why is there a minus behind that A?" my mother demanded. "Why can't it be an A or an A+?" she yelled. With each word, I cringed and wilted a little more. I wanted the bad feelings to stop and was determined to try harder. I'm sure that there were many successes, awards, and gold stars through my childhood. Glowing feedback from teachers on the bits of work that survives from that time, shows the reality. Yet I found it hard to savor the success; I only focused on my failures. I buried any negative emotions and drove myself to be better.

I collected my gold stars—editor of the school paper, high school valedictorian, a degree from Stanford University and multiple offers from technology companies for my first job. I started on my path up the corporate ladder, relentlessly seeking success, looking for the next raise and promotion, and switching companies quickly when that was the fastest path to my desired destination.

The achievement monster was briefly sated. The little girl who was scared of letting her parents down had been soothed, her fear silenced by my armor of success. I was a fierce warrior in the tech world and in design studios, as the advisor and creative director to top global brands. As a woman in tech, I learned how to act and be successful in a man's world. There was no place for mistakes or emotions if you wanted to be the best, or so I believed. I was succeeding in feeding the monster. But Silicon Valley was a difficult place to keep pace with expectations. The goal posts were always moving; it's a recipe for burnout.

You don't have to have the same childhood experience as mine to relate to the achievement monster. How we cope through our youth becomes our engrained patterns of identity through adulthood. We were taught and conditioned in how to define success. Being able to name this ambition as my "achievement monster" helped me quiet her voice. I can recognize when she's helpful, as she pushes me through a milestone, and I can start to hear when she is being unreasonably demanding. The monster is separate from me.

Each of my clients has their own achievement monster who drives them to do more. Naming, hearing, and visualizing this self-critic makes it easier to identify when they appear in your life. Some examples from my clients:

- Know-it-all Hermione from Harry Potter
- A looming large man with a stick named The Expector
- Spock from Star Trek, trying to eliminate all emotions
- Sister Francis, continually disappointed at all efforts
- Marge Simpson pursing her lips at every blunder
- A sarcastic popular girl named Heather who smirks that you'll never fit in

EXPERIMENT:
WHO'S YOUR ACHIEVEMENT MONSTER?

We all have an internal, self-critical voice that keeps driving us to unhealthy, unsustainable behaviors. Use these exercises to bring your achievement monster to life.

1. **Capture your first response to what your self-critic says when...**
   - You make a mistake
   - You want to speak up with an unpopular opinion
   - You receive challenging feedback
   - You start a new job

2. **Bring this self-critic to life.**
   - What does your self-critic look like?
   - What do they sound like?
   - Do they have a name?

3. **Think about what your self-critic is trying to protect you from.**

4. **How are they inadvertently harming you?**

Naming this self-critic and visualizing what they say helps you to recognize when they appear in your life. You can decide if you want to listen to the critic or make a different choice.

THE DESIRE TO LAUNCH PERFECT PRODUCTS

I've been part of teams that have launched many products. It can be a frightening experience, especially when it's the very first version of a new product or service. As the voice of design, I was often the person who said that we weren't ready, that we hadn't yet met the quality standards of a professional design worthy of a household-name brand. "It's going to be people's first impression of us, and we want it to be a good one," I'd argue. My gut—or was it my fear?—told the team that we had many deeper issues below the surface-level visuals. We may have created a brilliant "golden path", the expected way that people would sign up, register, and use the product, or perhaps express their opinion on a topic. Yet maybe we *hadn't* found this fantastic solution. *Perhaps there were actually three or four ideal paths and we've only defined one*, I'd worry. Perhaps we knew that there were points of confusion along the way and we hadn't completely removed all possible friction. *There's so much more to do*, I would think. *We could add a sense of beauty and delight by finessing the visual design, improve the illustrations, or create better animations to make the product feel happier and more fun to use.* The achievement monster inside me would transform into a fierce woman cracking her cat o' nine tails whip— yikes!—and say: "Keep on grinding to make it better. It's not perfect yet. ROAR." But she was wrong. The stark reality is that in ninety-five-percent of these cases, we were completely ready to launch.

Reid Hoffman, best known as a co-creator of LinkedIn, once said, "If you are not embarrassed by the first version of your product, you've launched too late." Reid was a graduate of the same interdisciplinary major program I'd studied at Stanford, Symbolic Systems. That program taught us how to think critically, be ethical, and consider both the human side as well as the technological underpinnings of the products we make. Reid's brilliant aphorism has become lore in Silicon Valley and has inspired many others including the famous Facebook value of "Move fast and break things." It emphasizes the first theme of speed: It's important to launch fast. In his article[1] on LinkedIn, Reid also shares two other themes:

"The second, less apparent theme, is that your assumptions about your customers, and how they'll use your product, won't be entirely correct. Eventually, you'll probably be embarrassed by how many wrong assumptions you made.

"The third theme is that you lose out by delaying the onset of the customer feedback loop: If you'd launched sooner, you would have started learning sooner. Instead, you launched too late. The word "embarrassed" plays a key role here."

In my experience, Reid's themes are accurate. From a business perspective, it makes sense to move faster. We all make assumptions about our various products, and we're often proven wrong. Time after time, even with my years of intuition and design sense, while our teams have created the best possible design solution, we're always surprised when real people start using the product in ways that we could never have anticipated.

But the most fascinating word to me in the quote above is *embarrassment*. This is a feeling of strong negative emotion and recognition of judgement, both self-judgement and fear of being judged by others. Many product people, especially founders, start to associate their sense of identity around the products that they release. In this all-encompassing intense world of technology, we work countless hours and often spend more of our free time, friendships, and non-work hours engrossed in the products we build. We are obsessed with discovering new solutions that will change the world. We want to have huge scale and impact yet working towards that vision of perfection makes it difficult to launch and release a product that's imperfect. But guess what? They all are.

We all fear judgement. We all fear making mistakes. Launch is when our baby gets released to the world, and we have no control over how others will respond. As Reid says, "You believe that you are going to be judged on your product—or even equated with it—so you want everything to be exactly right upon the initial unveiling."

This is where embarrassment comes in. As product creators, we can't anticipate everything. We will never be able to make it perfect. Fear and embarrassment are a critical part of the journey.

Launching products for decades has helped me realize the truth that Reid shared. Those statements normalized the achievement monster that I'd been feeding. I used the structures of iteration in product releases to fuel my experiments; Get moving, do it fast, and then learn from it.

I feel this a lot when I'm working on a personal creative project such as my portfolio. When designers interview, our portfolio is more important than a resume. This portfolio is a walk-through of case studies and work that we've accomplished with a dash of individual personality to answer questions such as, "What drives you?" or "What makes you different?" We are putting our entire professional identity into this slide deck and it feels vulnerable as hell. We want to show off our achievements in the best light. We want to polish it and make it better before we show it to the world. Our portfolio is our baby; it carries our creative DNA. The fear that others will think our baby is ugly holds us back.

We will never be able
to make it perfect. Fear
and embarrassment
are a critical part of the
journey.

I've learned that no matter how many times I go through this process, it's uncomfortable to share the work. There's always so much more I wish that I had done. What helps is knowing that I feel this same embarrassment and fear every single time. We want others to praise our achievements and to agree that our baby is the most beautiful baby that has ever been born. We want the praise, the positive external feedback of our achievement. And we all fear falling short.

Three or four jobs before I worked at Facebook, I started the mobile innovation arm of a traditional financial institution. I'd worked to build a physical space where designers had their own desks secluded from the rest of the business, as well as whiteboards, couches, and expansive walls where they could print out and put up the work. It was a space where everyone was welcome to drop in and co-create. One day, our executive sponsor walked into the space, and watched us work for a while. We were in the middle of a brainstorm and knowing his desire to not disrupt the process, I had the team carry on. He quietly walked over to a large whiteboard and wrote in large letters Steve Jobs' famous quote: "Real artists ship."

I remember being irritated at the time: *He's distracting from my brainstorm!* I thought. A little later, though, after having some time to reflect, I realized that he was giving me this same lesson on perfection. We weren't artists funded by patrons or galleries, who could endlessly refine for years. Instead, we needed to ship the products and get them out into the world, even though they weren't yet perfect. You too can experiment with shipping projects at work that aren't perfect. What if you shared the report early to get feedback rather than waiting until it felt one-hundred-percent accurate? What if you made a voice memo or video for someone rather than obsessing over that perfect email? It's okay to be nervous and uncomfortable, just try it!

THE FIRST TIME I WAS FIRED

The first time that I was fired, my "amazing leader who could hold it all together" façade was shattered. From 2006-2013, I worked for consulting firms that supported other companies. My last consulting job was for a Seattle-based development firm that coded products for clients. They wanted to move more into the strategic spaces of product and design. I'd worked with them on projects before, and I truly enjoyed spending time with the founders—we had similar values and visions. I joined them in a dual role that felt like a perfect fit for my ambitions. It fed my achievement monster a high-calorie diet. I was Head of Design *and* General Manager of the company's brand-new San Francisco studio. I threw myself into the role, working hard on both business development and client projects, as well as bringing design culture and thinking into what had previously been an engineering company. I also got to flex my operational muscles by searching for the location of the new San Francisco office space. On top of that, I was the first and only woman to hold a leadership position in the company. I got energy from the work. I enjoyed winning new clients and working on unusual blends of hardware and software projects. I was riding high on these client wins and the visibility of my perfect dual job. It felt like I was leaning into two different strengths as well as my personal desires and managing to make it all work. Anyone who looked at me would have admired how wonderfully I seemed to balance it all and my seemingly glamorous life of travel and cutting-edge projects.

Underneath the armor though, I was barely holding on. I had two daughters under five. While they were accustomed to their mom working long hours, this was different. I had an apartment in Seattle and was staying there two-three nights a week in addition to the required travel to client sites. One of my daughters, only knowing that this mysterious "Seattle" was the competitor that was hogging all her Mama's time, would often declare: "I hate Seattle. Seattle is bad."

I was working around the clock trying to drum up business for our new San Francisco office in addition to servicing the existing clients. I was also in a fierce conflict with another member of the leadership team who seemed to feel challenged by a strong-willed woman. These conflicts and microaggressions made my days miserable. In addition, with all the travel, I wasn't sleeping well, eating well, or exercising.

A year later, it seemed that pace might be finally letting up. The other member of the leadership team was no longer with the company. My then-husband, daughters and I headed off to a wonderful week-long vacation in Sayulita, Mexico with my best friend's family. Between us we had four little girls, who all squealed in excitement about staying together in a villa with a pool right on the beach. My husband and I briefly reconnected through surfing warm water. It was rare for us to spend this much time together—our growing distance was a downside of the achievement monster—and I got to spend many wonderful hours simply talking to my adult friends. We wandered around barefoot, enjoying the warmth, and the company. Enveloped by the sea-salt smell and slow ambling pace of the people around us, I was able to relax. I spent my days eating ceviche from beach vendors and buying fresh-cut flowers from the mercados. I felt relieved that playing with the kids was fun again, and not a nightly parental chore.

The day after we got home, both my daughters developed a stomach bug. They were in agony, endlessly throwing up in-between desperate dashes to use the potty. After my week away, the Seattle company's CEO and COO urgently needed to talk to me. I gamely hopped on a video call while keeping one eye on my miserable little girls. In a haze of shock, I listened as they told me that they had taken another look at the company financials and had decided to shut down the San Francisco office. I was being let go. They needed me to tell everyone in the San Francisco office that they were out of a job. I had never been fired before. I knew that it was supposed to feel like a colossal failure. That achievement monster was going to eat me alive. Yet surprisingly, something different emerged from this space. Even amid losing my job and the maternal ache of caring for my daughters, I felt a giant rush of relief.

I was aware that I had been holding up a house of cards, trying to make it all work. I was trying to be the perfect Head of Design, the perfect San Francisco General Manager, and the perfect mom. Of course, deep down, I knew I wasn't doing any of these well. It wasn't sustainable. I had set myself up for failure by doing two jobs for the company. I was stretched out way too thin. I was putting my family at risk and missing valuable time with my young girls. The week earlier in Sayulita, with surf and friends, had reminded me of the calm that had been missing from the previous year.

Of course, that feeling of relief and spaciousness didn't last.

In my typical pragmatic and high-achieving mode, I shut off all my emotions and set to work. I needed to find a way out of our building lease. I needed to figure out a plan for the remaining designers up in Seattle and make sure that my successor would be supported through the coming months. I needed to negotiate the best exit packages for the San Francisco team. And most agonizingly, I needed to communicate the news to each team member and help them find their next jobs. That last part wasn't my job, but I felt personally responsible. I had recruited and hired them. I fell back into feeding the achievement monster because I felt driven to complete this exit from the company with grace. I never questioned that it was my role to do so. I had no space to reflect or question my assumptions.

I'd tried meditation on and off over the past year at a suggestion from my coach to build in more reflection to my busy days, but the practice had never stuck. Yet this time, some inner knowing—perhaps the source of my relief?—desperately craved solitude. I spent the first day of unemployment at Spirit Rock, a meditation retreat center a couple of hours north of San Francisco. I was in silence for a lot of the day, either indoors with the teacher or outside walking the beautiful northern California hills in a slow, ambling meditation. I could see the dry pale grass undulating in the wind. Hawks lazily flew overhead, while lizards darted between the rocks at my feet. My long-suppressed emotions erupted. I wept. I re-hashed past conversations and yelled at the COO. I blamed the CEO for not hiring a salesperson. Mostly, I blamed myself for failing. I had trouble staying with my breath. Each thought brought my mind back to what I could have done better. But I kept going. As I slowly walked the hills, I felt my shoulders dropping, my jaw unclenching, and my anxiety fading away to stillness. Inside, I settled into the hours of meditation. I still had trouble staying with my breath. I reset back to my breath each time my monkey-mind whirled away. Surrounded by fellow silence-seekers, as the hours passed, nothing outside this space seemed to matter. For perhaps a minute at a time, I felt at peace and able to focus on my breath. I didn't need to speak, move quickly, or prove myself to anyone else. I was simply another person savoring the space of silence.

I reminded myself of that initial sensation of relief and how blessed I was in the space of having no responsibilities to an office, employees, or corporate expectations. For that single day at the retreat center, I didn't have to strive or achieve. I didn't have to be a mom. I was no longer responsible for the design practice or the San Francisco office. I was free to simply *be* in this temporary reprieve. I had the space to be free from the achievement monster for one day.

Months later, I was able to look back with deep gratitude for having been fired and released from the expectations of doing two jobs—a futile task to begin with, especially with my impossibly high standards. I wouldn't have been able to do it for myself, so I was grateful for the external push.

You don't have to have been fired to see yourself in this story. Those moments when we're caught up feeding the achievement monster can feel all-consuming. It's difficult to see the way out. I had believed I was doing the right thing. I kept going because I was afraid of saying no, afraid of slowing down, afraid of backing off from this prestigious job. Being fired had been my deepest fear, yet with the space of Spirit Rock I felt freed by it. I started to ask myself: *What matters most in my next job? What do I want to achieve for me, and not for someone else? How might I find the people and company who value me as I am? What if I could slow down?"*

Perhaps unwilling space has also been forced upon you, or perhaps my story can give you permission to slow down. I've learned how to support clients to transition out of unwinnable work situations, or to discover what's next for them after being fired. Relief has been a consistent emotion that reminds all of us that the path of the achievement monster always has been, and always will be, unsustainable.

EXPERIMENT:
PLAY WITH YOUR FEARS

You don't have to be fired or experience an embarrassing launch to break free of the achievement monster. Instead, consider this exercise. If you like to process through writing, pick up a pen and journal. If you're more of a thinker, consider these prompts when you're in a calm state; perhaps during a walk outside or when taking a shower.

Think about one area in your work or life right now where you are striving for perfection and afraid of not achieving. For many of my clients, it's reaching a particular role or title at work. For others it's getting a 'yes' from the right investor or receiving an offer from the dream company. It could be the next product launch. Or something completely different in your life.

Imagine the worst-case scenario, and ask yourself these questions:

- What's the absolute worst thing that could happen?
  - What are you most afraid of?

- Imagine that the worse-case scenario comes to be. What does it feel like the day you hear the negative news?
  - How do you tell someone else about it? Perhaps a family member, a mentor, or a friend.

- Think about waking up the next morning. What's the first thing you do after you get out of bed?

- Imagine that it's three months later. Now, how do you feel?

You might feel abject terror right now. You can write it down, take a break and come back to it later—or never if it's too triggering. If this exercise feels okay, consider your worst-case scenario. What were you most afraid of? Did the fear shift at all? Is there a different way you might approach the problem? Does it shed light on what truly matters to you?

MOVING FROM PERFECT PRESENTATIONS TO "YES, AND..."

I was stiff and awkward in my first improv session. We'd just been given some absurd prompt from one of our teachers. Our small group worked together to build upon the prompt. You never contradict what the previous performer said. Instead, you listen, choose one part of what they said, and build upon it. You say "Yes" to their idea, no matter how silly, and then choose to spontaneously add to it for the audience's entertainment. But I couldn't do it. I froze and didn't know what to do or say next. Many of my colleagues were in the same boat, nervously laughing as we caught each other's eyes. Our teachers tried something different. They asked us to repeat the scene in different styles—as if we were Texan cowboys, then debutantes at a sorority rush, then finally acting out a telenovela. The telenovela style finally freed me from my stilted participation. It was so silly, so ridiculous that I became a hapless TV housewife discovering that her philandering husband had an identical twin. I flowed into the histrionics, smoothly in sync with the other performers, at least for the duration of that scene. It felt liberating to let go.

In contrast to the spontaneity of "Yes, and...," I had a carefully controlled approach to my decades of giving talks, leading workshops, and hosting design sprints. I had always followed the same formula— sketch an outline of the talk in rough blocks, translate the points into slides, design a gorgeous deck, and build out the design while populating the talk content. Then I would rehearse the content, often running through the talk twenty-plus times until I was satisfied with the language and rhythm. I even enjoyed the process of giving a pecha-kucha talk, which is a 20 x 20 format where you have twenty slides that auto-advance every twenty seconds. To nail it, you must rehearse meticulously so that your talking points are crisp and match the pace of the twenty second slide advance. It's an exhausting ritual of endless rehearsals, made slightly more palatable when your entire presentation is under seven minutes. For both pecha-kucha and keynote talks, I would aim for the effortless knowing of the content that comes after intense memorization and internalization of the talking points. It felt like achievement. The monster was happy.

But this approach was time-consuming and exhausting. Continually aiming for a perfect presentation, often is. While I loved being onstage and the energy of giving the talk, I started to dread the extensive planning. The weeks of preparation in pursuit of perfection were both tedious and draining.

This carefully planned approach to talks was a mirror of my former controlling leadership style. I believed that I had to achieve it all and greatly exceed all expectations by a wide margin. I needed to be confident, prepared, and meticulously detail-oriented. Which really meant that I was massively over-prepared and obsessively controlling about every aspect of the experience. As you can imagine, this resulted in a lot of stress and inevitable panic when something went slightly off course, whether that was a crashed laptop, A/V issues, or the co-presenter showing up late.

This past year, I've been able to embrace more spontaneity and the spirit of "Yes, and…" from improv, with a little help from the COVID-19 pandemic. After March 2020, when in-person events were cancelled and everything moved to Zoom, it really didn't seem worth it to put in the time and effort for keynote-style, perfectly executed talks without the energy of a room of people. I started experiments to incorporate more improvisation into presentations. Instead of perfect slides, I tried planning out a rough outline of content to share and stories to tell. I'm still typically over-prepared—usually about half my content plan doesn't get used.

The first time I did this was nerve-wracking. It was strange to begin without the familiar crutch of slides and bullets. I felt anxious and unprepared, with butterflies in my stomach. I would freeze for what seemed like long minutes. But once I took a breath and got going, bit by bit, it felt better. I eased into the content that I knew so well, and my confidence grew. I experimented with giving talks with co-teachers where we blended our styles. I had to adjust to my colleague Jim Herman's talent for turning everything into a joke. I tried building upon his humor (Yes, and…) with a playful tone and an exaggerated eye-roll to poke fun at my own frustration. I learned to let other equally opinionated leaders flesh out talking points with less direction from me. I learned to tell stories and focus on the emotional intention of how I wanted people to feel after they listened to the talk. I learned to slow down, to play with gentle self-deprecating humor, and to release the pressure of being the "teacher" by opening up the conversation to more interactions with the audience.

Today, I focus on the shared experience of teaching a session and learning together, rather than the beautifully crafted story arc of my slides. Perfection has been replaced by planned messiness. Especially when I channel that dramatic telenovela housewife.

"PEOPLE WILL FORGET WHAT YOU SAID, PEOPLE WILL FORGET WHAT YOU DID, BUT PEOPLE WILL NEVER FORGET HOW YOU MADE THEM FEEL."

– MAYA ANGELOU

I learned to loosen up, to trust the process, and to believe that together, the audience, the other teachers and I, could co-create and participate in a unique shared experience. Zoom gave me the permission I needed to break free from the constraints of perfectly executed talks. After the first few, I stopped needing the comfort and security of my slides. I approached talks as casual chats with a spirit of curiosity and fun. I had made space for talks to be spontaneous, instead of being tethered to my idea of perfection in a gorgeously designed slide deck.

EXPERIMENT:
TRY IMPROV OVER CONTROL IN MEETINGS

Consider how you might let go of perfection in your meetings and presentations. What's your typical style of approaching a room full of people?

- Do you spend hours crafting the slide deck or doing meticulously detailed research around the position that you're going to present?

- Do you plan out every single minute of the sixty-minute meeting? What happens when someone else derails your perfect agenda?

Instead, give yourself permission to let go of this impossible level of control. Pick one of these three strategies to try:

STRATEGY 1: "YES, AND..."

Have you ever done something spontaneous that felt amazing?" Try bringing that feeling into your presentations. When someone derails your meeting, don't be irritated. Instead, take a few minutes to say, "Yes, and..." then build upon their train of thought. You can time-limit this "distraction" to five minutes and see where it takes you. At the end of the five minutes you can choose to: A) Summarize where you're at and return to your previous point, or B) See if you like where the meeting conversation has moved to and keep going.

STRATEGY 2: CHOOSE YOUR OWN RATING

The next time you're preparing a presentation, use some ratings to experiment with the level of perfection.

- First, ask yourself what your typical pattern is. On a 1-10 scale, how perfect is your typical presentation.

- Next, set a target for how messy you'd like to be. If your typical presentations are a 9/10 in finesse, see what it feels like to aim for a 7/10 in finesse, or challenge yourself to go for a 5/10.

Remember the 80/20 rule, also known as the Pareto Principle, which states that 80 percent of the outcome comes from 20 percent of the work. Maybe you only need to go for a 2/10 finesse? As long as it's the perfect 20 percent, right?

STRATEGY 3: PLAY WITH MEETING PROPORTION

How much of your meeting time do you typically map out in a minute-by-minute agenda? Try this strategy to increase more free-form time in a meeting. For example, if you typically fill up every minute of an hour-long meeting, instead try leaving fifteen minutes open for something freeform. It could be fifteen minutes of Question & Answer. It could be what's top on people's minds. And if no one says anything, then end the meeting fifteen minutes early.

CLIENT STORY:
THE JUDGEMENT OF OTHERS

Imani was a serial entrepreneur. A talented engineering lead, she had written the code for many tech company's most popular social features and was obsessed with doing things the right way. Along with her part-time day job which she calls "a breeze in the park", she was the founder of a business-to-business (B2B) start-up that saved people time by automating common tasks. A quiet leader, Imani struggled with self-promotion—it simply didn't seem right to talk about herself and her product. She wanted coaching to get out of her own way, as well as to learn the skills required to promote her company.

Imani shared with me: "I don't know if this product is good. I have a deep fear of judgement. Talking about myself and the company is hard. I don't think that the product is ready. The fear is that others will judge me and say: This is crap. This is too simple. This is not useful."

Working together, we came up with several intentionally messy experiments in which Imani would share an imperfect product. She tried recording a training video showing how different people used the product. In casual conversations, she made time to drop in talking points about why she started a company and what it did. She asked everyone she met if she could give them a demo of the imperfect pre-Minimum Viable Product (MVP). Imani practiced telling herself: "Of course, the product isn't perfect, no product ever is. I want to hear what other people think of it, both the good and the bad. Any information or knowledge is helpful."

This was not an easy process for Imani. Each experiment pushed her out of her comfort zone, and she kept facing her fear of being judged. Imani was afraid of people questioning her decision to found a start-up rather than continue working full-time at a tech corporation. She was afraid of people telling her that the product was terrible. And most of all, she was afraid that she'd been wasting years of her life. Throughout this process, the fear never went away. Yet the more she practiced, the easier it became. About four months into these active experiments, Imani admitted that talking to people about her company and product now felt natural, that she was starting to enjoy the conversations. "The asks don't seem like a big deal now," she said. "I now care less about how others will react and focus more on the learning."

Once Imani acknowledged her fear of judgement, she was able to move forward. The process was uncomfortable and messy. She took one step at a time. Eventually, after many months, she was comfortable enough with talking about herself and her company to start looking for funding from seed investors.

MAKING SPACE FOR MESSINESS AND FAILURE

We all make mistakes. Recognize and acknowledge the universality of mistakes. I make them. You make them. Your CEO or investors make them. That recognition and acknowledgement help to mitigate unrealistic expectations of yourself, especially the first time you do something. Instead of beating yourself up over these mistakes, accept that you've made them, learn from them, and even actively **celebrate** them!

The Japanese art of kintsugi involves repairing broken pottery by meticulously piecing it back together using liquid gold to both bond the broken pieces and enhance the appearance of the breaks. Each pottery piece becomes a unique work of art. The scars from the mistakes get turned into a beautiful new object. Kintsugi is a metaphor for how we can move away from the relentless pursuit of unattainably high standards. Build in experimentation, trust the process, and celebrate that the mistakes we make are an integral part of our authentic leadership. Owning and celebrating the mistakes makes us more beautiful and valuable.

Build in experimentation, trust the process, and celebrate that the mistakes we make are an integral part of our authentic leadership. Owning and celebrating the mistakes makes us more beautiful and valuable.

A fellow design leader, Andy Polaine, wrote on his blog[2] that we're all trying to break free of our personal escape room and I've never been able to forget that metaphor. We spend the first two or three decades of our life creating the perfect vision of what people have told us we should want. At first, it might be easy to collect the gold stars and follow the carefully prescribed path to a 4.0 GPA. Once we start working, there are clear expectations on how we're supposed to show up at work. There's a conventional path to rise up the career ladder. We keep moving blindly, fueled by fear. We've constructed this windowless, hermetically sealed room to hold us in place.

Then when something shatters our world, either a disaster or the desire to achieve something bigger, better, **more**, we realize that we can't get out. It can take us months or years investigating the clues that created these patterns, experimenting with different ways out. Beginning to name the fear and realizing that perfection can be limiting allows us to try many experiments within this escape room.

Space provides us freedom from the need to achieve unrealistic goals. Through my early years as a surfer, I believed that I needed to always push myself to ride the next best wave. Over time, I've learned to appreciate the pause, the exhale, and the pure enjoyment of being part of the ocean ecosystem. I once had the opportunity to ride the "perfect wave" at a manmade wave pool at the Surf Ranch in Lemoore, California created by the eleven-time world surfing champion, Kelly Slater. While it was truly an amazing wave, and one of the best rides of my life, it was too perfect and manufactured. In the ocean, each wave that comes will be different, a mixture of the different swells and complexity in the wind and wave patterns. Each ride is unique, so even if you fall while trying to carve a turn, it's still a great ride. There's always another wave. Like surfing, making space to lead celebrates both the fantastic ideas and the mistakes. In the creative process, a mistake is something to welcome. It's the opportunity to take the idea in a different direction, to learn from the mistake, and to welcome the beauty in the mistake which creates an even more beautiful outcome, one we never could have planned.

RESEARCH INQUIRY:
RE-DEFINE YOUR RELATIONSHIP TO ACHIEVEMENT

If you have your own personal achievement monster, start asking yourself the following questions to reset the relationship. Try to approach the questions with curiosity. Experiment with how you answer the questions: try writing in a journal, recording voice memos, typing into a device, imagining answers when you're on a hike, or chatting with a friend.

- What have been the major external achievements in your life so far? How would you outline these in a series of bullet points for a bio or introduction at a keynote?

  ○ Capture all the "gold stars" our culture tells us to value (e.g. awards, prizes, and promotions)

- What are your biggest "failures" or "mistakes"?

  ○ Consider how long ago they happened and what your current relationship is to the mistake. For example, do you focus on what you learned from them, or is there a pang of regret?

- What achievements are you proudest of? What has brought you the most joy or energy? Consider what feels like a good achievement for yourself and not for someone else (e.g. asking your partner to get married, mentoring a team member to her greatest growth, launching your biggest product)

- Who were you doing each of these activities for?

  ○ It could be for yourself, or for people in your work or home lives.

- Where do you judge yourself for not doing more? Which other people do you judge? Which people do you never judge?

- How might you achieve even more if you allowed room for messiness or mistakes?

Consider these questions as a starting point to explore how to re-create a new relationship with internal and external achievements. Go back and revisit the first part of this chapter, and try the experiment around Playing with Your Fears or Trying Improv. But first, see what opens up when you make the space to ask these questions.

CHAPTER THREE

DISTRACTED BY SHINY OBJECTS

I am a person who likes beginnings. I'm drawn to possibility, to excitement, and to the unknown. All of these traits come together most strongly with the energy of starting something new. Some of this restless energy comes from the nomadic nature of my childhood. My father was Thai Airway's growth guy, responsible for testing out new markets to see if the Thai public was ready to regularly travel a particular route. Although I was born in Singapore, we also lived in Amsterdam, Hong Kong, Bangkok and Seattle before I completed high school in New Delhi. Once on my own, I lived in California for university, except for six months in an exchange program at Oxford University.

For the most part, I loved moving countries. It opened me to new possibilities and let me leave anything unpleasant behind—friends I didn't really like, my Hermione-like school identity or labels that were attached to me like "teacher's pet." Instead, I could envision the next shiny opportunity ahead.

As humans we're driven by the next dopamine hit, whether from social media likes, tasting the menu at the latest restaurant in town, or discovering a glamorous little-known vacation spot. Well, those examples are my regular dopamine hits. I feel anticipation and excitement when I'm about to experience newness. I'd always felt that rush when moving to a new country, yet there's also a dark side.

The pull of always moving can make it impossible to rest and be content with what's happening right now. At times, I've moved simply for the sake of moving towards the next shiny object. Yes, what's present is interesting, but could there be something better happening somewhere else? This fear of missing out can drive us endlessly forward. We multitask between small urgent interruptions and never focus enough to go deep on something that really matters. Staying still can feel uncomfortable and complicated, but is moving to the next shiny object an avoidance tactic? The grass seems greener in the next field over, but is it really?

Making space for the present moment allows a little breathing room. It lets us dive deeper and wonder if it might be okay for us to slow down and savor where we are, the project we're working on. We have the ability to decide if we want to move forward and intentionally choose the next thing, or if we want to say no to the distraction of shiny objects.

DON'T MISTAKE MOTION FOR PROGRESS

Facebook has an Analog Research Lab (ARL) with dedicated staff and artists-in-residence. The ARL at its simplest is a physical place with printing presses and equipment designed to create analog objects in the real world, as opposed to the digital apps that most people associate with Facebook. The ARL's most known art are posters depicting sayings that reflect company culture such as "Be Bold" or "Focus on Impact." Some more recent posters show a shift in company culture as it has matured over the years. "What would you do if you weren't afraid?" promotes a sense of risk-taking so that the now-successful company doesn't get complacent. "Ship Love" reflects empathy, quality and a customer-centric mindset. While some of these can feel like top-down proclamations, many posters are made by individuals with a genuine desire to express their voices through creativity and art. The company walls are covered with these posters. Different ones get screen-printed each week and it's often a fun team event to co-create posters and bond over the manual labor of pressing down hard to screen-print each copy.

The poster that I think of the most, one of my favorites, is an arresting shade of bright red with the dark outline of a child's rocking horse in the foreground. Bold, all-caps, white letters state: "Don't mistake motion for progress," and it's attributed to "Jeremy's dad."

Are we simply rocking back and forth while continuing to stay still in one place or are we truly making significant progress?

As we experience shiny new objects and start new things, it's difficult to tell if our motion is movement. Are we simply rocking back and forth while continuing to stay still in one place or are we truly making significant progress? In the moment, the distinction between the two is often not clear. What's important is that we continue to be aware of when we are repeating the same shiny object pattern and remaining stuck in one place on the rocking horse. Starting to recognize and question the pattern opens up the possibility of uncovering insights that lead to progress.

DREAMING UP FUTURES FOR THE WORLD'S TOP BRANDS

Before I was fired for the first time, and three jobs before Facebook, I worked at a design firm for five years. It felt like a dream job (yes, there's a trend here!). When the world's top brands got stuck figuring out what was next for their business, they came to us. We were visionaries. We dreamed up the future of mobile computing, connected TVs, social networks, autonomous vehicles, and connected homes. We lived on a diet of adrenaline, shiny new ideas, and the thrill of presenting them to an audience hungry to be told what's next.

We typically had six to twelve weeks to work with a new client. They would come to us and share information about their business space, the people currently using their products, and where the company hoped to go in the future. After doing some hasty research, we'd start. I was the creative director, responsible for the client relationship and quality of concepts that our team delivered. I'd typically design a process to ensure maximum creativity in a constrained time frame. We assembled a top-notch team of world-class creatives—designers of all types with expertise in brand, strategy, content, systems thinking, research, visual, user interface/user experience (UI/UX), and motion. Everyone shared the core of unshakable commitment to generating new ideas and visualizing multiple new futures for our clients. We felt like the A-team coming to save the world. We did our best work under compressed time pressure and loved the stagecraft of painting what the world would be like in three, five or ten year's time, when people's lives would be improved with the client's latest TV interface, mobile phone, or smart refrigerator.

I loved it all. The time pressure, the anguish of wondering if we'd come up with something new, the self-doubt of wondering if it could possibly be good, and the performance of unveiling our three directions to the client before guiding them to the one that would best serve both their audience and business needs.

But most of all, I was addicted to the newness of working with a different client every two to three months. Each kickoff was like a beautifully wrapped jewelry box waiting to reveal its treasures to us. There was so much possibility and anticipation. One project might be wrapped in pleated floral origami paper with a satin ribbon tied into the perfect bow on top—a beautiful concept with not much meat behind it. One might be a giant cardboard box promising huge impact to the re-imagining and transforming of a business sector. One might be the robin's egg blue Tiffany box with the hope of romance and connecting people in meaningful ways. One might be a long, flat unknown parcel, from which you know a jack-in-the-box will pop up at you unexpectedly, but you wait in a state of deferred suspense and apprehension for when it will surprise you.

What I loved most about these shiny new projects was the kickoff meeting. We would get to sink our teeth and problem-solving minds into a new space. Everything was glowing—the clients sounded knowledgeable and earnest, the business needs were well thought through, and the audience definitely needed our help and expertise. We weren't yet into the messy middle where we'd get stuck with creative blocks, clients who kept changing their minds, or draining all-nighters to complete a concept we hated. We hadn't yet encountered the disappointing endings where I'd be talking to a high-powered corporate lawyer on a Saturday morning to persuade him that we were not in breach of contract, hoping that the contract I'd personally written, before we had the budget for our own lawyers, would protect us. It was the beginning, and beginnings are always full of optimism and possibility. I didn't yet have to deal with responsibility and could proudly wear my rose-colored glasses and imagine this beautiful future.

Jumping into the first shiny new object that comes along is like catching the first wave in a surf session instead of patiently waiting for the best wave for you at that moment. We may be dazzled by the possibility: a dream job or a perfect client that we hope will yield that elusive award-winning design or novel patent invention. And it might. Yet the dream we envision is in a bubble, devoid of the messiness of reality. When reality eventually hits—as it always does—sometimes it's easier to move on to the next shiny object and avoid dealing with the unpleasantness of missed deadlines, unhappy people, difficult conversations, discomfort, and disagreement.

CLIENT STORY:
FINDING MEANING BEYOND THE RESTLESS

I've known one of my clients, Chido, for over a decade. In his early career, he switched jobs every year. Each new job, he was sure, was the next amazing experience. Wherever he was currently working was the dream job until something shinier came along. Working at a virtual reality hardware company gave him the thrill of developing new ways for humans to interact with technology. Working at Apple gave him the experience of worshipping at the altar of Steve Jobs and having a leadership team that truly obsessed over quality and design. Working at a business software company allowed him to support people who had the motivation to interact with his designs while at work. Working for an entertainment company allowed him the joy of designing for fun and leisure. And so, it went.

As a first-generation immigrant from Southern Africa, Chido had come to school in the United States. Starting school in another country, especially with the big American dream of endless possibilities, sets you up to dream bigger and reach for the next sparkling opportunity. He had been bullied as a child, raised in a place where strong, powerful men were applauded, and he never felt like he belonged. He kept looking for the next thing to try, the next place that would be different, whether it was a new country, city, or job. Like I had been at the design firm, Chido felt that he had to keep moving, keep trying to find a place to belong.

Chido came to me when he felt stuck at his former job. He was smart and introspective, aware of his pattern of restlessness. It felt like he'd been "waddling around" aimlessly repeating some of the same mistakes for years. He wanted his work to be meaningful and give him a sense of purpose. He repeatedly started new jobs, at first feeling energized, then inevitably disappointed. His personal life was richer—he'd gotten married, had two beautiful children, and ended up leaving the fast-paced San Francisco Bay Area to settle in a small Midwestern town near his in-laws. Physically away from the hustle and grind of Silicon Valley, he found more space to slow down and think.

When work-from-home possibilities opened up with the pandemic in 2020, he stopped seeking excitement in new jobs. Instead, he returned to a familiar place—a stable business software company where he'd previously worked—returning to a team where he enjoyed the coworkers, the products, and had a supportive boss. His needs for newness and excitement were fulfilled in other aspects of his life, from becoming a dad to exploring his entrepreneurship with a side hustle.

In one of our conversations, we made space for him to dream about what experiences would truly be deep and meaningful. We visualized a future state of fulfillment near the end of his life. He saw himself as a hermit, living simply and apart from the burdens of humanity. He had a break from the need to keep moving and finding new things to do. He was living a simple life focused on personal design projects and mentoring others. Working together, we created a plan to achieve this future vision right now. He found ways to experiment with making more time for his creative projects. He started writing more to share his knowledge. He took on mentees so that he could teach and guide others. He focused on the present, going deep on what he needed for his side hustle, for his children, and also to share his path with others. Focusing on this present-state helped satisfy that restless feeling of newness and looking for the next shiny object.

Focusing on this present-state helped satisfy that restless feeling of newness and looking for the next shiny object.

THE GRIT AND FOCUS OF START-UP MVPS
(MINIMAL VIABLE PRODUCT NOT MOST VALUABLE PLAYER)

As for me, years of repeating my familiar distracting patterns helped me realize that I wanted more than shiny objects. In the middle of my career, two jobs before Facebook, I had worked for three different design consulting companies, starting new projects for countless clients. The thrill of kickoff meetings was starting to wear thin. I had stopped believing in the possibilities and was starting to get cynical because I encountered the same problems repeatedly. Many things we worked on only came to life in our imaginations. In one company, I had worked on over thirty future-facing client projects but only two had ever made it to launch and into the hands of real people. One of them, a social phone, combining innovative hardware and software, went on the market for two weeks before Microsoft decided to kill it. The project was a victim of poor execution and internal politics.

I was getting disillusioned with the glitter of kicking off new client projects. It felt like I'd been eating cotton candy, chocolate, and milkshakes for a decade and I craved the solid hearty meal of a perfectly-grilled steak atop a bed of microgreens. I was done with all the pretty distractions. Instead of breadth, I craved depth. I wanted to work on a product end-to-end, from the very beginning of its creation, all the way through product launch and beyond, with the subsequent multiple iterations. I wanted to go deep, come up with a solution for people's needs, and keep iterating to make it better. Rather than imagining new concepts, I wanted the pragmatism of running experiments with the products to see how much they helped people. Ideas were cheap and plentiful. I needed to see what happened when we took these ideas down a path of reality.

This led me to join a Series B-funded start-up in the big data space. We dug deep into problems faced by businesses that needed to deal with the volume of big data in the world, but without enough trained data scientists to show them how. Instead, we created a self-service solution so that any businessperson could answer their own questions, and work with big data as easily as using an excel spreadsheet. In the interview process, it felt like I already belonged there; I was deeply present and spent hours sketching ideas on the white board with both the CEO and the head of product.

I joined them as an early employee and head of design. Over the following two years, I played many roles and was able to try new things—and sometimes fail—very quickly. Without anyone else to do so, I ran marketing and built the company website. I created culture, values, and processes for the different teams. I built up a core research and design team that had equal input to product and engineering, a rarity for design teams in tech companies. We launched the first version, the bare-bones minimum viable product (MVP), and then two more versions over the next year through a process of experimentation and iteration. It wasn't brand new, shiny work. Instead, I felt deeply fulfilled by diving into intimate knowledge about an industry, the people who were involved and their very real problems that we helped to solve. It felt gratifying to hear how using our product saved them weeks of work. It felt rewarding when someone shared how empowered they felt to work with big data themselves rather than having to wait for a data scientist to crunch the numbers. I felt a sense of belonging, of being fully present and committed to a company, an industry, and a set of people all unified with a common mission.

In addition to the product, life at the company was both dynamic and fulfilling. We learned how to grow a company from ten people to two-hundred. We had to develop new processes and scale the team while keeping core culture and values intact. We hired up multiple teams and went through searches to find a new professional CEO, as well as heads of sales and marketing. It wasn't about finding new shiny objects but polishing the jewel we already had in place. Through collaborating with a strong team, I had found another type of meaning. At design firms, I felt like a performer, waving around smoke and mirrors to construct an elaborate story of the future that had no meat behind it. It didn't feel like I was serving anyone other than middle managers trying to spend their budget on superficial vision videos to pretty-up their dry presentations.

At that start-up, I learned the lesson of going deep versus broad. I felt confident that I could dedicate years to understanding a problem deeply and then solving it repeatedly, making it better each time. I saw the value of becoming the expert in a field rather than the consultant who danced around surface problems. I felt the same satisfaction I get from weeding an entire garden bed to let the kale and carrots seedlings grow, or from painting a room of the house and seeing the results of my labor months and years later.

It wasn't about finding new shiny objects but polishing the jewel we already had in place.

At Facebook, I continued this professional journey and spent multiple years digging deeply into a problem. While I continued to be excited by possibility and newness, I also felt the need to see projects through to a certain level of focus and completion. I found that I was able to both start new conceptual projects for an existing brand, and see them through rapid launches and iterations—my ideal integration of shiny new objects and focused longevity.

THE RESTLESS SABOTEUR

In my professional life, I was learning to slow down and go deeper into the problem spaces instead of being continually on the move to the next job. It was far harder to see that, in my personal life, my workaholic tendencies were the shiny new object distracting me from what mattered in my life. I wasn't able to make space until it was forced upon me.

Three impactful events of my life kick-started a multiple year period of introspection. Over the course of a year, in 2018-2019, my father-in-law passed, my marriage fell apart, and my father's health declined quickly until he too passed away. While the introspection continues, the space forced upon me in the wake of these events inspired me to leave corporate life to start my leadership coaching business. I started to question my compulsion to be busy all the time, my workaholic tendencies, and the relentless climb up the ladder. After my father's death, I spent months exploring how I could support others. First, I dedicated more time to running workshops and women's groups within Facebook; then I branched out to get more training to become a coach.

In the first year of running my own business, I discovered one of my most influential teachers. Shirzad Chamine is a New York Times bestselling author and creator of Positive Intelligence[1], a mental fitness framework to improve performance, enhance relationships, and live a more fulfilled life. My entryway to understanding mental fitness came through an assessment of the ways that we self-sabotage. I had never explicitly named all the voices of doubt and judgement in my head. For the first time, this framework gave me insight into naming my saboteurs. One of my strongest saboteurs is the Restless.

"RESTLESS, CONSTANTLY IN SEARCH OF GREATER EXCITEMENT IN THE NEXT ACTIVITY OR CONSTANT BUSYNESS. RARELY AT PEACE OR CONTENT WITH THE CURRENT ACTIVITY"

– POSITIVE INTELLIGENCE[2]

This was a transformative learning. I had never thought that having a magpie-like yearning for shiny objects could be a bad thing. I thought it was simply a part of my nomadic childhood identity and the trait that drove me to keep growing and pushing myself to be better. Yes, I'd had the insight that I no longer wanted to be in the shiny object world of kicking off new projects every couple of months. Yes, I'd switched my career into more depth of product work at start-ups and at Facebook. But I hadn't yet realized that this insatiable yearning to do more was a distraction from dealing with feelings of unfulfillment in my present life.

Some years ago, I had been Enneagram tested and came out as an Enneagram Seven, The Enthusiast. I remember the description:

"Generally, Sevens are excitable, spontaneous, curious, optimistic, eager, outgoing, future-oriented, adventurous, variety-seeking, quick, and talkative[3]."

I do have high energy and vitality. I am naturally curious, open, and spontaneous, ready and willing to drop what's currently happening and jump into adventure. I was interested in a breadth of activities and pursuits. I thought that I was uniquely positioned to keep going and reaching for the next big thing at work. I spent so much time reaching for it that I neglected to spend time with and honor the things I already had—my husband, my children, family and friends.

The shadow side of this Enneagram Seven became clear as I worked with Shirzad's Positive Intelligence framework. I learned that the Restless saboteur was an abuse of my natural strengths. I was running towards greater excitement in search of the next activity, seeking more space and meaning in my life, but it wasn't working. This was the final click! I could only find fulfillment, focus, and space by being in the present and seeing something through with deep focus. I needed the depth in addition to the breadth I kept seeking.

This shifted everything.

Looking back at my work history, I could appreciate the beauty of what I had at the start-up and at Facebook. In my business, I started to say no to the countless scaling activities ahead of me—launch a podcast, teach a new course, partner with these organizations, learn more about marketing, etc. It helped me to say "no for now," leaving the possibility that I might come back to them later. Saying no to all these possible distractions meant that I was saying yes to the things that brought me joy. I was saying yes to the 1-1 clients I was working with, to the partners in my group programs, to writing, and to surfing.

I only understood what I was going through with the benefit of hindsight, introspection, and tools like the Enneagram and saboteur assessment. I didn't automatically understand, even though I wanted to. My learning is part of this book and continues through my life everyday. You don't have to have experienced the loss of a parent figure or a messy divorce to relate to this. These moments of insight can happen more gently. You can choose to say no to a shiny new object. When you say no, you double down more deeply. You're saying yes to what you currently have.

EXPERIMENT:
USE ASSESSMENTS TO
UNDERSTAND YOUR LEADERSHIP NOW

There are many strengths-based personality assessments including Meyers Briggs Type Indicator, DISC, and Clifton Strengths Finder. They all give you different insights into your style and personality. The two I referenced in this chapter are ones that I find particularly insightful to learn about motivations/behaviors and saboteurs. Try them as an experiment:

- You can find many enneagram assessments.
  Most experts I know recommend this low-cost option:
  https://www.integrative9.com/getyourtype/

- Shirzad Chamine's Positive Intelligence self-sabotage assessment is free: https://www.positiveintelligence.com/assessments/

MAKING SPACE TO BE PRESENT TODAY

While my childhood was nomadic, today I live in San Francisco and have been in the same place for fourteen years. After my divorce, I remained in the house that we had bought together when I was pregnant with our first daughter. We had toured multiple places with our realtor when I was in my second trimester before buying the one that I deeply wanted. I felt the urge to nest. I wanted a place where I could bring home a baby and create a home for our little family. Throughout the years, especially when I was hyper-focused on growing my career, I felt trapped in one city. We would take three or four weeks of vacation each year in an attempt to satisfy my need for motion and adventure. And it was glorious. It's hard to be unhappy when you're distracted by vacations in a fabulous new country. Yet, after eleven years in this house, now with two children, I also needed to confront that I wasn't happy in my marriage. We were going through the motions of running the Taygerly Family Inc Partners in Parenting together, but with very little romance left. I felt trapped in the life I'd created and trapped in this house where I'd been in one place for the longest period of life. My marriage dissolved when we dove into six months of counseling to explore the stuckness.

In the early days of the separation, I indulged in my go-to pattern of distraction, I dreamed of a life where I could take my daughters away to a new place. It didn't matter where. I could have moved to any shiny new city: Singapore, Hong Kong, London, or Berlin. I soon realized that this was pure fantasy—I couldn't deprive my girls of living in the same city as both of their parents. I settled back into my home and resigned myself to living in San Francisco.

Given time and space, something shifted within me. A couple of years after my divorce, while I was sitting on the back deck, between the swaying birch tree branches and the shade of the pink almond blossom tree, I found myself curiously satisfied. I didn't wish that I was elsewhere. My ex and I were far better co-parents than we had been romantic partners. We had managed to create a new version of family. For the first time, I was comfortable to be still, to stay in one place, my haven in this beautiful city of San Francisco.

My constant motion, need for adventure, and the Enthusiast seeking variety and new possibilities are all parts of me. There had been stages of my career where I needed breadth. Working at a design studio allowed me to see a variety of trends and to develop the creative muscle to find solutions in many different ways. Later, I found value and fulfillment by going deep in the serious and pragmatic field of big data. There, design could serve business needs and launch meaningful products that were of value to real users. By going deep, I created long-term relationships with work partners, and experimented with different ways of building a team as well as culture and processes.

By going deep, Chido learned balance. He stopped moving from shiny job to shiny job trying to find meaning through work. He found meaning by settling down and having children, through working on his own creative start-up in his spare time, and through giving back by mentoring and teaching others about his path.

In the aftermath of my divorce, I found the space to examine what type of romantic partnership and life I truly wanted. It hadn't been enough to run an efficient co-parenting corporation, bonded by the love of our daughters, and punctuated by international trips to exotic vacation destinations. I examined my work, considering my three-hour daily commute against the support my daughters needed and wondering how much longer I could wrestle with the ethics of working at an advertising-supported social media company. Ultimately, I left that job and transitioned to a new career. Within this space of professional contentment, I was able to slow down and realize how happy I was to be deeply invested for fourteen years in one house in one city. It felt good to ground myself in the present. To slow down and go deep. My wish for you is that this story will give you permission to slow down and savor what you currently have in the present.

RESEARCH INQUIRY:
YOUR RELATIONSHIP WITH THE PRESENT

Every one of us has some feeling of being restless, even if it's not one of our primary drivers. It could be found in the yearning for the next job or vacation. It could be found when sitting quietly at home on a Friday night, wondering what everyone else is doing. Explore your relationship with being present and consider these questions:

- Are you in motion for the sake of motion—remember that rocking horse!—or are you moving somewhere meaningful?
  - If you don't know, consider how you feel. Is there impatience and anxiety, or are you deeply present and enjoying the process of motion?

- What matters most about that next shiny possibility? What do you hope to be different about it? What do you believe you will get from it that you don't have in the present?

- Are you stuck in repeated patterns? What is the pattern and how long has it been happening?

- Is your pattern one of constant motion for a period of time?
  - If so, try an experiment to slow down and focus on your day-to-day activities in the present.

- Is there a way to consider your restlessness as a strength? Perhaps you could find variety in going deeper and broader within a project rather than jumping to the next shiny activity.

Consider these a place to explore contentment with the present and the desire for change. Both aspects are often present at the same time. Notice your patterns and start considering what experiments you might create to try something different. If you're stuck, go back to earlier in this chapter and take the assessments to see if they shift anything.

CHAPTER FOUR

THE DISCOMFORT OF NOT KNOWING

I am a planner. I like to have a clear goal, a North Star that guides the dreams of where all the different aspects of my life—professional, romance, family, physical environment, personal growth—are heading. These goals give me a sense of security, a semblance of order and control within the messiness of life. I'm well aware that controlling all these things is impossible, yet I still yearn for it.

Being in the space of not knowing, with its fuzzy undefined shades of gray, makes me anxious. I'm on edge, anticipating that something bad is about to happen. It's a defense mechanism. I cover myself with armor to ward off murky future pain, instead of letting myself feel the possibility. *No thank you*, I tell myself. I'd rather know that something is an exciting 'Yes' or even a definitive 'No' than wait in the not-knowing. Waiting feels too passive, as though I'm giving up control. It's difficult for me to be patient, to take things one moment at a time and trust that the next step will unfold.

Yet, there can be peace when the future is not yet set or written. It's customary to start the design process without knowing where you're going to end up, or if you'll have an innovative idea. Then, inevitably, when you trust the process, you eventually make your way to a fantastic solution. It works every single time. As a designer, I've learned to be comfortable with this unknown. As a surfer, I know that every session in the water is different. It's virtually impossible to plan a surf session around the perfect conditions, even though many of us still keep trying. Making space involves leaning into this discomfort of not knowing. This liminal space is familiar to me in the product-making world yet far less familiar when I'm doing something completely new to me, such as writing a book, entering a new relationship, or forging a path as an entrepreneur.

It's deeply amusing to me that on the surface, I seem like someone who is good with the unknown. Some people would look at me in admiration and say, "I could never be creative or a designer," because it seems hard to make something from nothing. But the reality is that I still struggle with uncertainty and the impatience of wanting to have a pre-set, clear plan A, and a handful of backup plans. What's helped me is my history—knowing that I've been able to use the design process to make products that never existed before. Making space for not knowing acknowledges that while it's deeply uncomfortable, emotional, and full of heart-pounding anxiety, I can breathe, slow down, and trust the process—in all aspects of my life.

THE AFTERMATH OF GRIEF AND DIVORCE

The aftermath of my father's death and my divorce was a tremendous space of uncertainty for me. The immediate days and weeks afterwards felt fine—in a crisis, I stay busy and do well. Through the shock, my sister and I moved into the rituals of a seven-day long Buddhist funeral practice, and through the details of untangling my father's finances within the confusing Thai legal system. Likewise, I'd mechanically moved through the process of divorce—separating our marriage financials and creating a 50/50 child custody schedule, while working a high-pressure job with a three-hour commute. The busyness of tasks and planning left zero room for emotional space, whether processing grief or adjusting to life as a single mom.

When I was sixteen years old, I moved halfway around the world from my parents' house to start college in America. Consequently, I was used to going months without seeing my dad. So when I returned to San Francisco after the funeral, my routine wasn't all that different. I could move through my days in a semblance of normalcy. The divorce was different. I'd been with my ex-husband since I was eighteen, and we had been living together for decades. Yet while I tried to fall back into the usual patterns of being busy and working hard, my body forced me into the space that I needed to process long-suppressed emotions. For almost a year, I woke up at 4:30 or 5 a.m. every single day. My dreams were vividly cycling through feelings of fear, rage, and intense sadness. I tried to whitewash the feelings and take a positive spin, but the emotions needed to emerge during this most desperately difficult period of my life. My body and subconscious dreams helped start the grieving process.

It was a huge period of unknowns, spanning years. I was able to move through it by getting through each day, one baby step at a time. It took longer than I ever imagined I would need. It took processing. I was kicking and screaming my way through it, but ultimately, I had to accept patience and take the space because there simply wasn't another way through.

CLIENT STORY:
KNOWN UNKNOWNS AND UNKNOWN UNKNOWNS

There are two concepts in product management of *known unknowns* and *unknown unknowns* which helps contextualize this ambiguity. *Known unknowns* typically refer to risks that you are aware of. When designing, we know that when we conduct user research and show real people the product for the first time, they will always point out things that we'd never thought of. These are the unknowns that we can plan for and count on happening, the *known unknowns*. *Unknown unknowns* are risks that you never see coming. COVID-19 was an *unknown unknown*. Yes, we'd seen swine flu and other variants of contagions, but very few people had anticipated or predicted the full extent to which a pandemic would disrupt the world.

The discomfort with new challenges, the personal *unknown unknowns*, was a pattern that I saw in my clients. One of my clients, Dimitri, worked for a company with a complex product and multiple audiences. He led the development effort across mobile and desktop. With the addition of a new Chief Technology Officer, the company needed to scale, moving from Dimitri's known world of mobile development to a web application where the software would be written once and used in multiple places from mobile phones to laptops. To jumpstart the scaling effort, the company hired an outsourced engineering team. This was a huge place of unknowns for Dimitri. He was used to being the mobile development expert.

Through the months we worked together, he struggled with trusting the external engineering team, because they weren't meeting his expectations of quality. It was an unknown group of people, in another country, selected by his bosses. He didn't have control. He simply had to roll with a decision he didn't completely agree with. Dimitri tried a number of different experiments to build more trust including setting up communication processes, discussing quality, and sitting down side-by-side over Zoom to do the work together. However, as the months passed, it became clear that trust wasn't the issue. Their code quality wasn't improving, but now Dimitri knew more about the subject matter. He moved away from a place of unknown unknowns. Some of his uncertainty and lack of trust came from not knowing the content of a new space. Now the problems still came up, but he knew what to do about them. He moved into a place of known unknowns and gained confidence in the new relationship, the technical space, and the process.

One of Dimitri's biggest insights came while he was renovating his apartment, using contractors for the first time. This was a project he had more control over. He chose to start the project and spend four weeks living in a hotel while his apartment was being worked on. Like the technical example, he didn't trust the contractor team and their level of quality AND he didn't understand the subject matter—materials, building codes, options for fixtures, paint choices, and other aspects of the renovation.

He had to move from a space of *unknown unknowns* about the people, the process, and the subject matter. Dimitri was deeply self-aware and immediately saw the parallels to his development work. In both scenarios, he saw that when he gained more knowledge about the process, it eased his anxiety, anger, and frustration.

It's easy for us to go inward and second-guess our decisions, conversations, and emotions when we're in a place of not knowing. Dimitri was insightful enough to recognize his patterns, acknowledge his discomfort, and while he didn't exactly enjoy it, he was able to learn and then choose to react in different ways. He could trust the process and recognize that as he gained more knowledge about the subject matter—both the technical code base and the renovations—he better understood the unknowns, which alleviated both the anxiety and discomfort.

Gaining more knowledge about the process eases anxiety, anger, and frustration.

CLIENT STORY:
WAITING TO HEAR BACK ABOUT AN INTERVIEW

A common situation of not knowing is job interviews. There's the active part of this process, where it feels like you're in control—making connections, having early conversations, sharing resumes, prepping for the multiple rounds of interviews, and finally conducting and experiencing the different conversations with the company representatives. Once you've done everything you can possibly do—from the prep-work before the meeting, being in the interview, and the requisite follow-ups afterwards—all you can do is wait. This can be a place of severe self-judgement that spirals down into second-guessing and anxiety:

- *Why did I give such a dumb answer to that question?*

- *I should have practiced the presentation more.*

- *I didn't really speak up and say what I meant to. I froze in the moment.*

- *I couldn't stop speaking so much and so fast. I should have slowed down to listen more.*

- *Did I give my opinion too strongly? Will it come off as being aggressive?*

In addition to the endless rumination, it feels like we **are** in a place of judgement. We're waiting to hear the other person or company tell us if they want us or not. If they say yes, then—magical rainbows!—we're headed to the perfect job. If they say no, then we believe we are talentless, rejected failures. We can get stuck in this thinking, waiting for someone else to pass judgement on this black and white view of ourselves.

One of my clients, Katherine, had worked at the same company for ten-plus years and now felt ready to look for a new job. She hadn't been interviewing during that entire time, so she had no practice and wasn't prepared to be in this dreadful place of waiting to hear back. This was a giant place of *unknown unknowns* for her. It led her into a spiral of anxiety around the interview process, and she wondered if anyone would ever hire her. She worried that the success she'd experienced in her current job was a lucky fluke.

One of my other clients, Yingshi, had had a twenty-plus year career and had gone through the interview process regularly every couple of years, whether or not she ended up moving companies. She was more practiced in the process, and while there was the same agonizing wait to hear judgement, Yingshi was familiar with it. She knew what it was and how it felt. While it still felt uncomfortable, she also knew that the anxiety would soon pass and that the judgement would not dominate her life forever. For Katherine, because it felt like the first time she'd interviewed, the discomfort of not knowing was agonizing and occupied most of her waking thoughts.

Brené Brown has a saying she refers to as FFTs[1]. FFTs are Fucking First Times. The first time you do anything is a new unknown to you. You're going to mess it up and make a ton of mistakes. It's going to feel uncomfortable because you've never done it before. You don't have models or patterns to refer to. And still we continue to put pressure on ourselves, especially my most high-performing clients, to do it correctly, to execute perfectly, despite the fact that it's our first time.

Having a name for this experience, that it's an FFT, helps to normalize the feeling of discomfort. The FFT is meant to be uncomfortable. To you, it's an *unknown unknown*, and as humans, we're wired to crave comfort, security, belonging, and knowing. Of course! Doing something new, or not knowing how to do something, or waiting to hear things develop and hear about a job... all of these are stages of not knowing.

My method of dealing with the discomfort was to create structure, leaning towards my innate desire to control my life. I wanted to control the big things—where to live, what to work on, and what the next one, three, or five years would look like. I also wanted to control the small things:

- *What should I eat for lunch?*
- *What show should I watch tonight?*
- *Do we want to go to this party?*
- *What time will we go to bed?*

Most of these can happen from the inside-out. We can decide what we want to do, and then plan for it. While I can't control what each surf session will be like, I can consistently plan to paddle out—rain or shine—

"It's perfectly normal
for something new
to be uncomfortable."

several days a week. With that structure of consistency, some sessions will have more memorable rides than others, however, I'm always out in the water. What's harder is the surprising forces from the outside-in that spin our world out of control. The COVID-19 pandemic is the prime example of an unexpected and unwanted force of nature that took away all control over where we go and who we see.

People, especially the ones we are closest to, take away our control. We can't control them. They won't do what we want them to, even though we clearly know best, or so I tell myself. They refuse to follow our neat plans for them. We get into conflict from this need to control others. And much of it also stems from fear—we want our own freedom and are afraid of being controlled by others.

I've come to realize that while it could be possible to control and plan out every aspect of my life, that's not what I really want. That life would be monastic and would be missing surprise, spontaneity, and the humanness of interacting with other people.

Making space in our lives gives more margin for error and spontaneity when things don't always go according to plan. Rather than expecting perfection, we can prepare for a normal imperfect day where the cat throws up on the rug as we're late running out the door for a crucial meeting. Making space—in our mental state as well as our calendars—helps us laugh when messiness and mistakes happen. It creates room for the unknown and the unexpected joy of following a serendipitous encounter.

CLIENT STORY:
MAKING PHYSICAL SPACE FOR CHANGE

Alexis had always followed a carefully organized career path. She had a degree from a well-known design school. After graduation, she'd worked at many of the name brands in Silicon Valley. She was fully in control and kept getting bigger titles, more responsibility, and bigger teams. She was a craftsperson, meticulously detail-oriented, and known for the hours she'd spend polishing a product until it was ready to launch. She was working at Apple, reveling in the joy of being at a company that shared her similar attitude to delivering high quality products.

Yet this well-planned life was starting to feel like a straitjacket. Alexis wondered if this was all there was to her career. Even though she had everything she'd ever wanted, it started to feel like it was "the consolation prize at the carnival, never the biggest main prize." Something was missing, she felt. Something was off.

Alexis decided that her family needed a change—a pivotal one. They needed to get out of the pressure cooker of the Bay Area, where it seemed that everyone was on a well-planned career path, climbing up the corporate ladder or launching their own start-up. She found it hard to breathe and think when surrounded by expectations and comparisons. Alexis and her family decided that Austin, Texas might be a better environment. The company would move her, and the move would shake things up. For the first time in her life, Alexis admitted, "I don't have a plan."

After spending time in Texas, Alexis realized that by abandoning her carefully structured career plan, she was able to let go of some of the need for control that had been driving her entire career. Being in Austin—the motto of which is "Keep Austin Weird"—gave her permission to be more authentic, even goofier. She spent almost a year in a period of reinvention during which there were no expectations to show up a certain way.

Alexis felt okay standing out. She identified with a platypus and its duck-like snout, not beholden to fitting into expectations of how she should be. With the space after the move, she realized how constraining her former life had been. She felt ready to explore different paths of creativity.

After running a number of experiments—*what if I do more writing? How might I share my knowledge? How can I evangelize design more? How could I help facilitate better communication?*—she realized that she loved creating and teaching workshops. She learned to let go of the detail-oriented perfection of delivering a product the Apple way. Instead, she embraced the messiness of teaching. No two workshops were ever the same. She could have an outline and prepped material, but each workshop would follow the energy and desires of each group of participants. She was energized and lit up in a way that she hadn't felt since the early years of her career.

Only within the physical change of moving to Texas and embracing the unknown was Alexis able to make space for goofiness and spontaneity—for fun!—in her life. In this new environment, she freed herself from her expectations of a tightly controlled career plan and found new meaning in her leadership.

MOVING FROM PROBLEM SOLVING TO HOLDING SPACE

Through the first decades of my career, I prided myself on being a problem solver. Give me a complex, ambiguous challenge, and I'll find the best way to solve it with a product or service that makes people's lives better. We designers identified people's unmet needs and provided an app to solve their problems, whether they wanted it or not. Sometimes we unwittingly created other unexpected problems. When rapidly launching features, we didn't anticipate that bad actors could use our product for unintended purposes.

Um…did I mention that I used to work at Facebook?

Risk. Bad actors. Unintended purposes of the platform. None of that mattered. We could always create another feature, another technology plan, another roadmap to keep pushing the platform forward. When I left the world of tech, where I'd always prided myself on having the plan and being the problem solver, it took me a while to learn that coaching is the opposite of problem solving.

"WE DO NOT COACH FOR A PROBLEM TO BE SOLVED, WE COACH FOR A LIFE TO BE LIVED."

—JIM PATTERSON

Jim Patterson was one of the early coaches and leaders at the Co-Active Training Institute[2]. I spent ten months in training with the Co-Active Training Institute to learn the craft of coaching. I had extensive experience teaching, speaking and mentoring people. I thought I knew how to coach, given that I'd been leading teams and running women's leadership workshops at Facebook for many years. But we don't know what we don't know until we jump into it. Remember those *unknown unknowns*?

With my product background, I approached coaching as problem solving. I wanted to help people solve their leadership problems as I'd helped businesses solve theirs—understand the space, uncover creative solutions, and make a plan. However, I repeatedly had to learn that the skills that made me a good problem-solver also made me a terrible coach.

Part of the coach certification process involved sharing recordings of my conversations—with the client's full permission—with a supervisor. The supervisor and I would watch the recordings and both assess how well I did against a matrix of coaching skills. In my first supervisor call, I thought I was hot shit. I'd been full-time coaching for months and my clients were getting fabulous results, or so I thought. During this session, I moved one client from his stuckness into finding a new experiment to try for his start-up's product/market fit. When she rated me on the matrix, my supervisor gave me an overall coaching score—three out of ten. I was devastated. To me, it was a score that fell far below a failing grade of 60 percent, and I didn't care that everyone I talked to later said this was normal.

My supervisor told me: "You're doing a fantastic job problem solving, you're getting to the next steps and outcomes. But that's not coaching. Stop telling him what to do."

Another one of my teachers reiterated: "Coach the person, not the issue."

As a natural problem solver, I knew how to plan. Research the context of the topic, experiment with a short-term solution, then try the next step. I told people how to do it, using directive language with emphatic statements of fact, drawing upon my extensive past knowledge and career experience. I was the expert, after all. I did a lot of talking, convincing, and selling. The skills that served me so well in my design career were undermining my ability to coach.

Gradually over the coming months, I began to understand what the instructors meant. In coaching, it's important for the client to find their own path. My job is to encourage, acknowledge, and celebrate the client taking the next small step towards their desired outcome. Yes, part of it can be suggesting the way, or co-creating it, but it's never solving their problems for them. I had to stop trying so hard to control someone else's life.

Instead, each coaching conversation is a three-part container where the client brings in a particular issue, we end with co-created experiments, and the magic happens in the free-form middle. The juicy middle is a meandering exploration of deep listening, powerful questions, embodiment, and ideation all wrapped up in a swirling soup of emotions. As a coach, I'm paying concentrated attention to the client's words, body language, emotions, and the unnameable space of what wasn't said. I've transitioned from being a designer of digital products to designing the process of holding human space.

As a leadership coach, I support my clients to become their most powerful selves: fulfilled leaders in their work and their lives. I honor them by not solving their problems—they are naturally creative, resourceful, and whole enough to design their own visions and solutions.

In becoming a coach, I freed myself from the pressure of having to have a plan. Rather than a problem solver, I became a guide, a confidant, and a truthful voice to make the observations that no-one else would dare to say out loud. I moved from planning into making space for playfulness and experimentation.

"IN IMPROVISATION, THERE ARE NO MISTAKES."

—MILES DAVIS

There are no mistakes in coaching, either. Holding space for a client allows them to be open to transformation in their life. Yes, there are still frameworks and structures. Through one lens, confronting fears and difficult truths can feel restrictive. Yet through a coaching lens, the discomfort expands to create space for brainstorming, diving deep into feelings, choosing new perspectives, and ending with the co-creation of an experiment. This experiment is the smallest possible next step to try on this journey of learning more. Similar to the design process, there is the opening of exploring multiple ideas and the focusing of choosing a direction.

I expanded my identity to be a coach who could make space for others. On many occasions, I do help clients with problem solving. For example, I work with women and people of color around salary negotiation. This is a very specific topic with rules, timing, and ways to react to the offer on the other side. In these situations, I problem solve AND I hold space for what really matters to them during the negotiation. I've learned to expand my identity to be someone who can help others at problem solving and transformation, doing and being.

How do you approach uncertainty, or the discomfort of not knowing in your own life? My default mode was to bear down harder and try to mitigate the unknown by creating a plan A, plan B, and plan C. Instead, I've now learned to take a looser, more flexible approach inspired by the design process of opening to many possibilities and then focusing on an experiment. And knowing that it still feels uncomfortable even when you trust the process.

HOW TO MAKE SPACE FOR NOT KNOWING

Ambiguity is hard. It feels easier to live in a simple world of right and wrong. I love my children's books and 19th-century English romance novels because I know what's going to happen. The good guys always win. The couple will get together and live happily ever after. That is a fantasy world of black and white. Our real lives and work have many shades of gray and multiple colors of the rainbow.

Dimitri learned that his negative emotions and anxiety would subside as he got more information about a new development process or renovating his apartment. He moved from *unknown unknowns* to *known unknowns*. Katherine recognized that since she hadn't interviewed for many years, she was out of practice. She told herself that interviewing was an FFT (Fucking First Time), that the discomfort of waiting to hear back was normal. Alexis was able to loosen her carefully laid out career plan and take a risk on a family move to Texas. She finally felt free to stand out and be weird. Each of them let go of a little control and in doing so, gained more comfort with ambiguity. They learned to take inspiration from their past to become more confident with not knowing the future.

The not-knowing lives inside spaciousness. It is the possibility before we have to make a decision or commit to a person, a job, a move, or a house. This space will be deeply uncomfortable when it's an FFT. Yet for areas of more familiarity, such as the design process in product creation, this space of not knowing is a deeply creative, generative place where all these possible visions for the product are all alive, and we don't yet have to commit or decide where to go. Reminding myself of truths I do know has helped me through the discomfort. Truths like:

1. **Doing something new, for the very first time, is difficult.** It's an unknown unknown to you. Make time to learn the space and allow yourself to make mistakes. It's the very first time, the only time you're going to get to be a novice and have a beginner's mind in this context. Many people who start surfing hate it. You spend so much time paddling and bobbing, and only very rarely might you even stand up on the board for a millisecond. Your arms and abdominals hurt from using new muscles. And it seems like you'll never be able to stand.

2. **Trust the process.** Have confidence that the process will unfold over time and gradually we will move from a place of not knowing, to some ideas, and then to a path forward. Time is our friend. I keep consistently paddling out for surf sessions no matter what the conditions are. The more practice you get, the more hours you spend, the better you get. Even if it's difficult to see the small changes along the way.

3. **Keep moving, one baby step at a time.** Not knowing can freeze us in paralysis and stasis. Instead, look to see what small experiment you could try next. Completing an action, no matter how small, moves the energy and possibility forward. Keep paddling for that next wave. Keep trying to stand up and hit that bottom turn.

I've learned to trust the process and take it one step at a time in my entrepreneurial business. I've become comfortable listening to the rhythms of my body and emotions as I wake up each morning and feeling into the unknown today. As each day passes, each new challenge will slowly move from being an *unknown unknown* to a *known unknown*.

FOCUSING EXPERIMENT: YOUR HISTORY OF OVERCOMING UNKNOWNS

As I keep reiterating, the design process is a cycle of divergence and convergence, opening up to multiple perspectives and then focusing on a small number of choices. Through the past chapters, you've examined some research inquiries which have broadened ways to look at busyness, perfect achievements, and shiny objects. Now, consider this experiment to focus on your past in order to better understand how you can work through future ambiguity.

1. **Start with an audit of the past.** Look at each major part of your life. You can break them into pre-adult, early adult, and then each decade of your life. Or you could also look through the lens of each job that you've held. Another option is to use life milestones such as graduation, jobs, home ownership, and relationships.

   For each phase of your life, when have you gone through times of deep uncertainty? Capture these. For each challenge, how did you overcome these *unknown unknowns*? When did you feel your best in these times? What were you doing? Who was there?

2. **Identify the facts of what is unknown right now.** For the different areas of your life, list out the challenges and areas of *known unknowns* that are bothering you.

   Some examples are, "I don't know …"

   - … if I can prevent type 2 diabetes by adjusting my diet
   - …whether my boss thinks I'm ready for a management position.
   - … if I will get an offer to buy out our company.
   - … whether my partner and I will stay together.
   - … if this project will launch on time.

3. **Identify the emotions underneath the unknown right now.** For example:

- I resent having to control my diet.
- I am afraid of being stuck in this same job and salary band forever.
- I am worried that we won't have a successful exit.
- I feel insecure and unworthy of this partnership.
- It will be my fault if this project isn't successful. I will be guilty of letting down the team.

Know that these negative emotions are normal. Naming emotions instead of suppressing them acknowledges that they exist. Naming them helps to integrate and manage the reality of these emotions. Name it to tame it.

4. **Now, build on the experiences of your past to create an action for how to move forward.** Find examples of how you've handled these types of unknowns before. Or if it's the first time you're tackling a new challenge, can you draw parallels from how you've handled other situations? For example:

- I was able to control my diet to lose weight before my wedding. I can try the same strategies to invest in my health.
- I did research and asked for my last salary increase. I can talk to more people.
- I empowered my team and delegated the right tasks to make our project successful. These skills will help us with this launch.

What small action do you want to try next?

Use your history of muddling through unknowns to remind yourself that you've done this before, and you can do it again. This process is a new experiment to help you focus and weather future unknowns. The solution to the anxiety evoked by unknowns is to make space for uncomfortable emotions and to move forward one baby step at a time, one day at a time.

CHAPTER FIVE

BREAKING OLD PATTERNS

We spend most of our lives settling into and creating patterns for how to survive and thrive in the world. My pattern is continual forward motion and being excited for the next shiny object. I've always presumed this was a product of the constant mobility from my nomadic childhood as a third culture kid—defined as people brought up in different cultures than that of their parents and raised in different environments during childhood. In the photograph of six-week-old me from my first passport, I see a chubby-cheeked, slightly confused baby held in my mother's arms. It was taken before my first flight from Singapore to Bangkok at four months old. Airplanes felt like my happy place. Flying was a magical, special occasion marking our movement to a somewhere new.

Airplanes were a place where I could comfortably be in the in-between space. It felt celebratory. We always dressed up to travel, my dad in his dark well-cut suit and my mom in a custom-tailored fashionable outfit. In a photo I found recently, I thought she looked like Jackie Onassis, with her wideset doe eyes, wavy dark hair, and little hat perched just so on her head. I was proud to put on my best clothes—a fancy dress (all little girls wore dresses), hair brushed to shine with pretty clips, and tights which bunched up at the ankles and made my legs look like wrinkly elephant skin. As a tiny child in my giant reclining seat, I set up my stuffed animals on both sides of the tray table and had fabulous tea parties. The flight attendants would stop by and give me extra treats. Some of them played with me in between their other work. I felt special. It was a place of safety and freedom. Airplanes were my transition space, a metal cabin up in the air where time didn't matter, rules didn't apply, and nothing bad could happen. Despite being the definition of in-motion, airplanes were a place of stability that existed outside of my pattern of continual motion.

PATTERNS BECOME OUR IDENTITY

We all have structures and patterns that we settle into. Our physical environment is the place we live in. It's set within the context of the city or country's cultural norms. We fall into the patterns of how we live our days including when we go to the grocery store or out to eat, and how we spend our leisure time. We may have regular times when we wake up and go to bed. We have morning routines for ourselves and daily rituals around caring for pets or chauffeuring kids to their activities. On a weekly basis, we build in other patterns—when we exercise, see friends, go on dates, or pursue other entertainment. We choose how to spend our weekends, either in exhausted relaxation after a heavy work week, a frenzy of chore completion, or filling it with activities we finally have time to do—that extended bike ride, that elaborate dinner party or late nights out dancing.

At work, we have a professional structure that establishes when we show up at work and when we leave. Increasingly in these always-connected times, we must practice establishing what non-sleeping hours are okay for work messages. These structures slowly become routines that we fall into. Repeating this structure each day makes it easier—we don't have to make a new decision each time. And as we repeat them week after week, they become unconscious patterns, like how we make the automatic drive of our daily commute without even knowing what happened on the road that day.

These patterns extend beyond the physical and environmental; they also include mental and behavioral patterns around our identity. We show up a certain way at work—professional, competent, with a certain work persona having our polished act together. And over the years of our career, these patterns wear into grooves which have changed us without our ever even being aware of it. We've settled into these roles of our work identity.

Some of us are "know-it-alls," quick to solve every problem around us. We take pride in being the smartest person in the room and are the first to offer up advice to others whether they want it or not. Others of us are the selfless volunteers. We want to see things done right. So, we jump in and do it ourselves. We tell ourselves that our team members don't do it properly, but the reality is it's simply: *Not how I would do it.* We need to pick up the slack, to redo the work, and to present it in just the **right way** (which really means our way). This jumping in is not completely altruistic—we think we know that it's the best thing for the team and company.

Others among us are used to being the quieter voices, the people pleasers who don't want to make a fuss and tend to flow with the consensus. It's easier that way. We don't want to make any waves. We would rather focus on the collaboration and harmony of the group. We continue to ignore the increasing resentment that comes with pushing down our opinions and keep thinking about the happy team dynamic. And most of us will vacillate among all these types depending on context—work versus home or friends versus family—and the people we're around.

These patterns become our identity, like my identity of being a traveler. We've spent years creating these work and personal personas. We've stopped questioning or thinking about them. They've settled into us like a comfortable wetsuit that stretches to accommodate repeated movement. We've spent years creating them and making our lives work well for us. There are also work comforts that we may not want to walk away from—a regular salary, solid routine, and the perks of free food and generous benefits that tech companies offer their workers. Mostly, it's a good life.

NOTICING THE CRACKS

Until one day, the wetsuit doesn't seem so comfortable. Perhaps it's started to get some holes for the cold water to seep in. Perhaps the zipper holding it together is starting to crack. Now, we start to notice discomfort within some of these comfortable patterns. There's a niggling feeling or negative emotion. Sometimes this is internally motivated. Perhaps we feel stuck and frustrated and are seeking a way out. Sometimes the cracks are externally motivated, based on events that happen to us and push us to jump into reactive crisis mode. Or perhaps a friend has told us that some aspect of our life feels worn out. It now feels like this identity

We've spent a lifetime creating these patterns that we thought we wanted, or the culture told us to want. And now it starts to feel like a strait jacket.

has become constraining. We've spent a lifetime creating these patterns that we thought we wanted, or the culture told us to want. And now it starts to feel like a strait jacket. Or that you're living someone else's dream, perhaps a parent's like my "tiger mom." Soraya, the overworked, overwhelmed player-coach engineer (from Chapter One), didn't want to be pigeonholed as the go-to person to solve everyone's problems. Perhaps our work patterns turned us into people we never wanted to be. This room we've meticulously constructed is too small. And locked. Now we're searching for a way out of our personal escape room. The solution is through recognizing old patterns and making space for change.

CLIENT STORY:
MOVING AWAY FROM PLEASING OTHERS

Soraya had been overwhelmed and consumed by busyness when we met her in Chapter One. She was leading key projects for her company and being pushed by her boss to take on more teams, more projects, and more leadership. She grew up wanting to keep the peace and make sure that everyone around her was happy. In her workplace, she kept saying yes. She became the key person that everyone—engineers, leadership, the front-line salespeople—looked to for answers. The success felt good, and it built up her confidence. But she was working around the clock and constantly felt like she was on the edge of burnout.

As we worked together, she started exploring what truly mattered to her. She was leading engineering teams focused on cutting-edge robotics. When there was a problem with the code or with one of the clients, everyone knew to call Soraya. She was the heroine always able to jump in and successfully firefight each problem. Yet while she enjoyed being known as this go-to person, she got increasingly resentful about doing everyone else's work. This resentment provided an opening to shift her pattern of people pleasing.

Over the months, Soraya started experimenting. She learned to watch for what work she truly enjoyed. Outside of work, she loved baking, designing videogames, and crafting meticulous nail art. She knew she was a creative problem solver and a maker at heart. Soraya enjoyed the making-space and finding the solution to hairy technology problems that no one else could crack. But she didn't want to do this for everyone. One focusing experiment that Soraya tried was to stop supporting multiple projects broadly and instead went deep with a single product team. For some months, she was assigned to work with a team in Asia, and that change temporarily fueled her. But when she returned to the U.S., there was still a feeling of dissatisfaction.

Ultimately, Soraya had to make space to wonder if she truly wanted to keep managing. Her manager wanted her to lead teams; yet being responsible for others activated her people pleaser side. She yearned for creative space and to eventually start her own business. Soraya didn't have a clear next step yet. She wasn't ready to quit managing or leave her corporate job. However, identifying her pattern opened the space. She was able to start experimenting with what next career move might mitigate the resentment that came from being the leader who came to everyone's rescue.

Soraya looked to her feelings of overwhelm and resentment as a self-initiated trigger to change her pattern. She had the choice—and her manager's full support—to explore different futures. She also explored physical space when she temporarily relocated to Asia. However, an international move isn't realistic for many people. Instead, let's consider looking to our vacations.

VACATIONS AS A PATTERN BREAK

Vacations are a commonplace pattern break. Many white-collar professionals have a mini-vacation each week, conventionally the two days that follow five days of work. But in our busy, always-on lives, work can bleed into all seven days. We need more than the weekend to replenish our energy. We've allowed the boundaries of these mini-vacations to blur and evaporate; many of us check into work throughout the weekend.

Only when we take a longer vacation, of a week or preferably two or three, do our bodies start to slow down. Now we truly feel a shift in the pattern. We notice what it's like to take a full exhale and feel relief from the pressures of work. On vacation, we stop obsessing about our boss, our other colleague who seems to deliberately get on our nerves, or the pressures to continue to deliver impactful work. Some of us may be able to disconnect fully and switch our work brains off. Some of us still occasionally check in and may never be able to truly stop worrying about work. Vacations are the space where we first taste how different life can be: slower and less compulsively planned. It's the perfect scenario to observe pattern breaks.

EXPERIMENT:
WHO ARE YOU ON VACATION?

Think about your last vacation or imagine a future dream vacation. Consider the patterns from your "regular" life that you're switching up.

- What were you craving when you picked this vacation destination? What brought you joy and energy? Perhaps it was rest and relaxation as a break from the busyness of life. Perhaps it was to go deeper into a hobby or activity (I often pick places with a good surf break). Perhaps it was to experience a new culture, unusual food, or a volunteer opportunity.

- What would be the perfect vacation day for you? Consider:

  ○ The time when you wake up and go to sleep

  ○ The planned activities versus free, spontaneous time in the day

  ○ What you eat and when you have meals

  ○ The people you spend time with and how you spend the time with them

  ○ Your energy levels when you wake up and throughout the day

  ○ The emotions that you feel. What brings you joy and contentment? What stresses you out? What gives you pleasure?

Observe these pattern breaks while on vacation. Is there any part of who you are on vacation that you want to bring back to your everyday life?

Vacations are a physical manifestation of making space. We can feel the space expanding around us. The space exists for all the emotions to bubble up, including the joy of experiencing something different. It's an experimental space. On vacation we can do things differently. This luxury exists because it's a space apart from to-do lists, busyness, and the problem-solving of regular life.

The toughest part of a vacation is re-entry. Many of us don't want to turn off emails and work communications when we're out of the office because we dread the pile of work that's waiting for us afterwards. I've seen some wise colleagues schedule some days or even a week of ease-back-in time where much of their day is blocked off from meetings. Set the boundaries you need for re-entry. Take the vacation, but don't undo the good of it all by diving back into work immediately. Instead, investigate the experiment and consider what aspects of the vacation you might want to carry back into everyday life. After a vacation, make space to transition back into "regular" life.

Whichever your approach, whether to re-enter slowly or by tearing the Band-Aid off, recognize that transitions are difficult for everyone. We can fall back into our old habits, run hard to catch up, and end up working many extra hours to compensate for the vacation days we "stole" from our work life. As you transition back, notice what's different. What do you want to keep with you from this pattern break?

OUR GLOBAL PANDEMIC EXPERIENCE

Vacations are an internally driven mechanism of breaking patterns. We choose how, when, and where we're going to take them. In contrast, everyone on the planet—together and individually—experienced an externally driven pattern break with COVID-19. The upheaval started in 2020 and continues through this book's publishing at the end of 2021.

2020 was a landmark year. The beginning featured a long period of uncertainty. We were unsure of the true extent of the coronavirus pandemic and inundated with conflicting messages from the authorities. *Should we wear masks? Should we quarantine our groceries at the front door for twenty-four-forty-eight hours? How much danger are we truly in?* We saw gruesome images from Italy of wrapped bodies and full mortuaries. Plans

After a vacation, make space to transition back into "regular" life.

were paused, rescheduled, then cancelled. We watched as what we knew of our previously normal lives went by the wayside. We said farewell to international trips. We missed family milestones, weddings, and funerals. Even the smallest parts of our days were different—we worked from home, settled into setting up a makeshift workspace and dealt with having our partners and roommates in close proximity—All. The. Time. Some of us were also working a second shift taking care of kids and acting as their distanced learning teachers. It was a long year. 2020 has been the largest external pattern break that many of us have experienced and it was very much unwelcome. Yet through the discomfort, pain, and uncertainty, it has brought space to many people. We had no other choice.

There was no need, and no time to name the patterns we were breaking or get curious about what was different. Instead, we were simply thrust into it. And after weeks or months of living wildly altered, socially distanced lives, some of us began to change. With the complexities of the outside world forcibly removed, we had to go inwards and find our sanity where we could. That is, for most of us who aren't essential workers or teachers who were consumed with supporting the rest of us through this crisis.

We slowed down and made more intimate connections with the people we lived with.

We valued the members of our extended pod, cherishing the brief times we could spend together.

We were forced to re-experience our work and our colleagues through a new lens.

We interacted with coworkers and friends outside of our pod on Zoom. It was exhausting to only experience our connections on a rectangular digital screen, never being able to make actual eye contact, while braced for unexpected interruptions from people and pets around us. Yet, we had the magic of teleportation, instantly flipping from meeting to meeting without a commute or room change. All while wearing sweatpants.

This was a period of great creativity for some people. Musicians recorded breakthrough albums, chefs mastered new recipes at home, and many of us finally had the time to explore long-postponed hobbies: baking, crafting, painting, writing, or simply relishing the extra time to be bored.

Banned from gyms, some of us were able to spend more time outside. This time in nature nourished our bodies, which were eager for movement after hours in front of a computer. It fed our minds looking to make sense in this time of upheaval. At state beaches, the parking lots and parks overflowed as many of us sought escape from the indoors. Several coastal counties, including San Mateo county just south of San Francisco, had to turn away visitors and impose fines or tickets on vehicles that were registered more than five miles away. They wanted to mitigate crowds and have the outdoor space available for locals to enjoy. I am lucky enough to live in San Francisco, right by Ocean Beach and beside plenty of local parks. I could continue surfing where we're naturally socially distanced in the lineup.

En masse, we learned that we could handle this external crisis, our first global pandemic, together. We didn't like it, but we adapted. We came to see that we are inherently resilient and adaptable. We formed new habits. Some will stick and some won't. We broke decades of pre-existing patterns. We were given time and space to reflect on systemic racism and how it has given rise to the culture we live and work in. And through the transition to a vaccinated world where things opened up more, we now have the choice to decide which patterns we like and want to keep. We've never had more choice than we do right now.

MAKING SPACE TO BREAK PATTERNS

For me, airplanes represent the timeless space between patterns. It's a space of play and experimentation without consequences. The examples from this chapter—Soraya choosing her own work over pleasing others, learning from our vacations, and the COVID-19 pandemic—help us with recognizing patterns. It's comfortable and normal to fall back into the same patterns. Some of these patterns are wonderful and work well for us. I've always used the space of airplanes to do my best creative thinking and long-term visioning. However, to move forward, we need to notice the patterns that have been holding us back. We need to intentionally make a choice to try something different.

$\bowtie\kern-0.6em\bowtie$

OPENING EXPERIMENT:
WHEEL OF LEADERSHIP

We all have patterns that we believe keep us safe—keeping busy with work, aiming for perfection, leaping to the next shiny object. If we want to create change, we must be willing to explore many facets of our life and leadership. In my Co-Active Coach Training[1] program, we used a technique to explore what matters called the Wheel of Life. I've developed my own version called the Wheel of Leadership to focus on aspects of both your life and leadership. You can use your ratings in each segment to explore which patterns you might be willing to change.

What's most important to this is not your level of success in each area of the wheel, but your level of satisfaction. Take a look at the wheel and each of the segments. On your personal scale of 1 to 10, mark how satisfied you are with each aspect of the wheel:

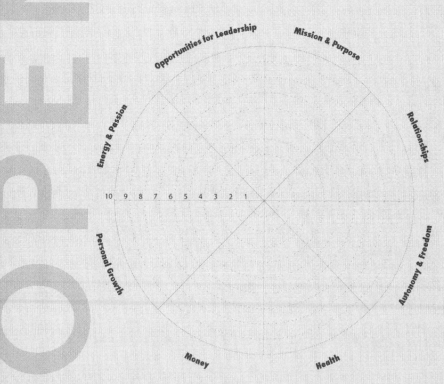

You can fill out this wheel in the context of your professional life, or you can expand it more broadly to look at the entirety of your life. Remember two key points:

1. This represents how you feel today.

Things can change on a dime. You could get into an argument with your boss, and the way that made you feel might drop your level of satisfaction in the Relationships segment. That's okay, it's a blip. To smooth out these blips, I recommend that you re-assess on this wheel every three months.

2. You are in control of your choices.

Your choices lead to the feeling of satisfaction that's captured on the wheel. There are many external uncontrollable factors in these segments. Even if you have faithfully applied sunscreen your entire life, you might still get skin cancer. You might join a company for its mission, yet after some months come to realize that the leadership didn't truly embody the mission. However, you can control the behaviors and choices that you make about your health and your job. You control your choices and satisfaction.

After looking at your wheel, ask yourself these questions:

- What ongoing patterns might be responsible for any low scores on the wheel?
- What ongoing patterns bring you joy and empowerment and fun?
- If you had to pick one segment to make a change, which one would it be? What's the pattern you'd like to break or enhance in that segment?

The Wheel of Leadership is an opening tool to help explore existing patterns across these segments. It helps you see areas of high satisfaction and contentment. It helps identify where you might be least satisfied and ready to break away from an existing pattern. Let's start experimenting!

CHAPTER SIX

UNDERSTANDING YOUR INTENSITY

I've always been an intense person. Part of this identity is believing my own story of being a difficult person. In the past couple of years, I've been revisiting this identity, both for myself and my clients, to understand who I am as a leader. I've felt like I was the difficult person through every single one of my corporate jobs. When I worked at Disney Interactive, a couple of jobs after graduation, my coworkers, several of whom I consider dear friends gave me the nickname of "Attitutti," and I only learned of this years later. I felt hurt and also a tiny bit of pride. Yes, I was full of attitude. It was a safe cover from which to operate. I was starting to find my voice by expressing my opinions loudly. It felt difficult to be a woman of color in tech. I'd suppressed much of my emotions trying to lead other people how I thought a leader should. This insecurity led me to shout with full expression so that I would be heard. It was a coping mechanism, an armored persona, that became a part of my leadership.

This intensity continued through my first decade of managing teams, mainly at design studios where this "tough as nails" persona and expectation for excellence as a Creative Director was valued. Confusingly, while my work was never questioned, I would get feedback on my "mixed signals" and "communication style." I was holding on to a tough persona where I felt like I had to be the expert, the commanding leader, and tell others what to do. I strongly valued high expectations for everyone around me, and most of all for myself. Yet, through the years, my secret fear was that nobody really liked me. I knew I was good at the work, but I wasn't confident about anything else. I felt torn. I knew I wasn't conforming to the standards of what was expected of a woman—to be quiet, to listen, to be respectful and give others their space.

It's only in the past two years that I've thought more about how being female and Asian affected how others perceived my leadership. I've identified as a feminist for decades. For most of my Stanford Computer Science classes and years working in tech, I've been the rare woman in rooms of men. Sexism was a familiar fight, racism less so. In tech, Asians had never been the minority. At Facebook, when we hired for underrepresented groups, we focused on women, African Americans, Latinx, Indigenous people, and people with a military background. Asians and whites were in the majority. I never felt like I experienced racism in my happy little tech bubble and continued as the model minority, never dreaming that my leadership struggles with intensity had anything related to unconscious bias of common expectations for an Asian female.

However, by any standards, I was intense. Often, when I heard someone else's idea, my first instinct was to put on the skeptical hat and ask many detailed questions. I sought to understand, so I told myself. But the reality is that my problem-solving "black hat[1]" wanted to find all the edge cases and explore why the idea might not work. Through years of feedback from trusted managers, I learned that my first blunt reaction to an idea could really turn people off and destroy their confidence, especially if it had been difficult for them to present the idea in the first place. We've all known people in meetings who regularly respond with a rebuttal. I was that person through most of my early career. Gradually over the years, I learned to replace the interrogation with curious inquiry, more like a compassionate friend. I learned to pause and acknowledge the best parts of an idea when I first heard it: "Yes, creating a mock infomercial about being a video creator moving from YouTube to Facebook can really bring to life the value of being on our platform." Then, I could seek to understand more about the idea by building it up with questions: "Tell me more about how we can envision the road map as a video?" And finally, move into brainstorming for how to build upon the idea: "Do you think we could combine this with Facebook Live?" I moved from a lawyer cross-examining the witness into an ally co-creating a direction. I was learning to adjust and build relationships with people rather than insist on the passion and vision of MY ideas.

It was many years later when I reached the breakthrough moment.

Honoring my values of growth, in 2018 I asked my manager at Facebook to send an anonymous survey out to people with the question "How much do you enjoy working with Tutti?" on a 1–10 scale. I was trying to resolve this feedback that had followed me through the years. It seemed so contradictory. I didn't know what to make of it, or what actions to take to "fix" myself. The survey results and the free-form text that accompanied it were illuminating. There was a huge polarization: small clusters of people rating working with me at a 1 and the large mass of others rating me at a 9 or 10.

This gave me a blinding flash of insight: Perhaps my intensity and challenge could be a good thing, a superpower that drew some people to me. I had never been able to see that before.

I pulled from memory, each specific piece of feedback that had followed me through my career in tech. The negative pole of feedback:

- *Aggressive and impatient. Dismissive of bad ideas. Feels like you're being interrogated. It's intimidating.*

- *She is too quick, confident, and competent in coming up with the right answer.*

- *Too intense. Too much for some people. Tends to let her emotions take over.*

The positive pole of feedback:

- *Tutti has X-ray vision and energy like a 5 year old.*

- *Tutti brings so much passion to the table. She is a clear, direct, and compassionate communicator, and this positive energy rubs off on the rest of the team.*

- *She isn't afraid to fight for the right thing to do. While it's not always comfortable, I do like that Tutti challenges us all to think more broadly or deeply about the problems being solved. She sets a huge vision and keeps us honest.*

Perhaps my intensity and challenge could be a good thing, a superpower that drew some people to me.

I realized that both poles—the negative and the positive—were true and that I had been excessively focused on "fixing" myself and changing myself into someone else. There's nothing wrong with being perceived as a difficult person. There can be an intense collection of big emotions inside, fuelled by a passion and vision for what needs to be done. You have strong opinions and believe in how beautiful your vision of the future is. You want it so badly because it'll be great for the business, the organization, and the people who will use your products. It feels like the right path, the North Star for us all to head towards.

And as a leader, you also need to know the impact of that intensity on all the different types of people around you. It's polarizing. Some people will adore you. They are more similar to you; direct communicators that thrive on challenge and competition. They've bought into the vision. They're the superfans already celebrating in the front row of the concert. They validate your ideas. They are the ones who remind you that there is true value and energy behind your passion. These are your people. It's important to find and know your biggest cheerleaders and fans.

You don't have to identify as a difficult person to relate to my story. Many of us have experienced this disconnect between the work we do and how we do it. It can be confusing when we are clearly doing high quality work, yet somehow there's a gap in communication or connection. The way to bridge this gap is through relationships.

We have to lead with inclusion, to build our relationships, to create a safe atmosphere of trust, and to make sure that everyone feels heard. Katherine, who we met in Chapter Four as she started to interview, had to face this lesson in her meteoric career rise.

CLIENT STORY:
STUCK IN HER DIFFICULT PERSON STORY

Katherine was a star in her globally distributed company that was shifting to modernize their decades-old enterprise software. Every product team she led did impeccable work. Their professionalism, speed, and ability to ship high quality products was incomparable in her company. Her handpicked team was equally brilliant, and they trusted her completely. Katherine was valued by her boss for being a

They're the superfans already celebrating in the front row of the concert... These are your people. It's important to find and know your biggest cheerleaders and fans.

truth-teller and for always knowing what the next step forward would be. He championed her to the leadership team and found the right opportunities to keep her learning. She kept abreast of industry trends, keeping her product thinking current to look out for opportunities the company could benefit from. Katherine was passionate about doing well for her boss, the company, and the people who used her products. Because she was focused on achieving her career milestones, she worked hard to win all these external successes. Katherine didn't stop to think about whether she liked the job, respected these leaders, or if they saw her unique leadership.

Katherine's stress and pressure to keep performing escalated as she climbed in the company. The size of her team doubled, then doubled again. She got more responsibility, bigger goals, and fewer people who understood her. The company was changing. Her boss left, and she lost her supportive anchor. The new teams she inherited didn't trust her. They didn't understand her cutting-edge ways and wanted to continue working as they always had. They wondered why they needed to pay attention to the latest industry trends. They believed that Katherine was different, that she wouldn't take the time to understand their perspective. Katherine's new teams came from more traditional backgrounds and were tied to their existing processes that had worked for decades. They weren't used to moving so fast and trying newer, agile ways of working. Her new boss expected her to continue her rock star trajectory, but she was too busy to support Katherine. She'd always had that support with her old boss who truly saw her and believed that she could drive change at the company. Now that he was gone, she felt the increasing pressure. Her new boss simply pointed out her deficiencies and wanted them fixed.

Her direct reports were going to her boss with complaints about her. She teetered on the edge of burnout, working harder yet feeling like a complete fraud. Her new boss, and teams, didn't care about her earlier successes; she decided that her prior brilliance must have been luck. She didn't know what to do, and she simply felt that she was too difficult, too intense for anyone to work with her, much less trust her as their leader.

When Katherine first came to me, she said, "I want to work on building more effective and inclusive relationships **and** not lose my personality completely in the process." She was self-critical and blamed herself: "Ninety percent of this has been a crippling identity crisis. I'm a terrible designer and a terrible woman (because designers and women are supposed to be great at empathy, right?)" She was trying to "fix" herself and adapt to be what the company and everyone else wanted her to be. She knew she was perceived as a difficult person.

She was ready to make a change but didn't know what it was.

Katherine and I worked together to better identify who she was as a leader. We co-created small experiments so she could take it one step at a time. She worked on revisiting the strengths she had exhibited in doubling her teams—her problem-solving acumen, mama-bear intensity while defending her teams, and the way she represented the customer perspective in strategic business conversations. She experimented with capturing her wins in a weekly note: the engineering teams, who trusted her, and the glowing feedback she received from people who used her product. She started to believe in her own leadership again. Over many months, Katherine re-built trust with the teams reporting to her, slowing down to listen to their individual stories and the pains that the re-organization was bringing them. She empathized with their challenges of working across time zones with colleagues at a main office in the east coast of the U.S., and multiple other offices across Europe and Asia. She practiced directness and relationship building with one boss. When she was re-organized yet again and was transferred to a new boss, she approached it with the excitement to build a new relationship and not the bitterness of another unwanted change.

During this time, Katherine started interviewing with other companies to create future opportunities for herself. This has been a new place of *unknown unknowns* (from Chapter Four) for her, and nevertheless she persisted. Many months into the interview process, she received feedback from a hiring manager. He clearly saw and named her strengths: "You're a change agent, able to connect engineering, product and design across a global team to get things done." This truthful commentary unlocked an insight. The things she'd been beating herself over—being obstinate about quality standards, moving too fast, not supporting her teams—dissipated in the face of her strengths as a passionate change agent.

Katherine had been stuck in a story she'd continually told herself: She was too intense, not empathic, and challenging. Being re-orged, having things not work perfectly with her new teams, and having an unsupportive boss led to her obsessing over her mistakes. The judgemental phrases she repeated to herself—*"They don't like it when I ask questions."*, *"I don't read people very well, and I tend to tell them the truth. It's too much."*—illustrated the influence of the story she had created.

The external interview feedback from that one hiring manager reminded Katherine that there wasn't anything wrong with being a passionate truth-teller. She didn't have to stay in the place of loneliness and self-blame. Instead, she could make small steps to re-build trust and relationships.

Katherine finally saw her own brilliance. She has a vision and the ability to advocate for her company's customers in a unique way that was key to modernizing their decades old enterprise software.

THE LONELINESS AND REGRET OF INTENSITY

Many of us are familiar with the myth of Icarus, who first experiences the joy of flight on wings made by his inventor father, Daedalus. Daedalus warns his son not to fly too high because the heat of the sun will melt the wax, and not to fly too low because the sea foam will soak the feathers. As we know, Icarus flies too close to the sun. The wax holding his wings together melts, and he plummets to his death in the ocean. This story is often used to warn us of the ego of humans trying to fly, of not heeding the warnings, and of being too ambitious. But for me Daedalus is the fascinating character. Years before his creation of wings, he'd been a master craftsman and genius inventor in Athens. Although he was skilled, the myth goes that he was intensely jealous and murdered his own nephew because he was fearful that the younger would become more skilled than he was. Banished to Crete, Daedalus became the craftsman to King

Minos. He continued to push the boundaries of his brilliance, helping the queen—cursed to fall in love with a bull—create a hollow wooden cow so realistic that it fooled the bull. With the queen hidden inside this creation, she conceived and birthed a half-human, half-bull minotaur. King Minos was enraged and forced Daedalus to construct an inescapable labyrinth for the minotaur. Upon completion of this labyrinth, he and his son were imprisoned for life at the top of the tallest tower on the island. This is when he invented the power of flight for Icarus and himself, leading to personal disaster. Upon his son's death, Daedalus lived the rest of his life in loneliness and regret, continuing to pay for his hubris.

While Daedalus does sound egotistical and wrapped up in his own brilliance, his mistake was not daring too greatly, as Brené Brown would say. His failure was not recognizing how important his relationships were. Many self-professed 'difficult' leaders are high performers, brilliant at their craft. They are visionary operators, indispensable to their organizations. They are also incredibly intelligent. Daedalus was obsessed with his inventions—he was the first person to facilitate the power of flight—but he let his ideas run roughshod over what he cared about the most, his son. Many leaders are willing to pay the cost of broken or lost relationships— with their teams, their partners, or their children—so that they can keep winning at their work and their ideas.

A relationship is a high price to pay. Pursuing inventions and visions at all costs is an incredibly lonely place to be. There are hidden, never-to-be-spoken regrets, and relentless shame. I feel for Daedalus, living the rest of his life without his son in endless self-recrimination. His ego and reputation were the outer armor to the loneliness inside.

I know this feeling because it's a familiar place for me, for Katherine and for many leaders I've worked with. My unrelenting focus on climbing the corporate ladder led to many years of placing my husband last on the priority list. It's one of the factors that led to our relationship becoming the Taygerly Family Inc Partners in Parenting and eventually, to divorce. It's only in the years afterwards, within the drive of creating my own business, have I been able to mitigate this continual intense push to do more by experimenting with prioritizing my relationships and giving myself permission to rest. Part of writing this book and its lessons is to remind myself to slow down and intentionally *Be* rather than continuing to *Do* more.

EXPERIMENT:
MAKE SPACE FOR REST

Many high achievers have a drive that keeps them doing and going constantly. This behavior can drive up our intensity levels and make us seem more "difficult" to people around us. One experiment is to prioritize rest. Rest is a key ingredient of physical fitness and training. Rest is also how to find creative breakthroughs for a sticky problem. Pick one of these strategies to experiment with:

1. **Schedule in regular rest time throughout your work week.** Build in exercise, a lunch break, or a tea-time break. You could try this once a week or more regularly in the days of your work week.

2. **Which of your relationships give you a sense of ease and rest?** Perhaps it's a true work friend with whom you could schedule regular one-on-ones. Perhaps you want to regularly grab coffee with a mentor or a mentee. Perhaps it's a regular night out with a group of friends or a phone date from the comfort of your couch. Seek out the relationships that bring you energy and joy.

3. **If you're working on an important project that involves new ideas and creativity, as your schedule permits, build in overnight rest time to let the work marinate.** When you come back to it in the morning, you'll be fresher and will view the work with a fresh perspective.

4. **When you're working towards a high-stakes deadline—perhaps an end-of-quarter close, a board meeting, or a key project launch—build in rest time afterwards.** Depending on how long this intensity has lasted, consider blocking the rest of the afternoon or taking the upcoming days off. Consider this post-deadline rest as sacred as the actual deadline itself.

One of my former colleagues would book herself a manicure after a day of back-to-back meetings to deliver performance feedback to her large team. Katherine added in a daily walk when she was most frustrated. As an experiment, implement one of the rest strategies today. Monitor and see how it makes you feel and if it improves your work quality.

FOCUS ON RELATIONSHIPS NOT IDEAS

One downside of this intensity is that we can be laser-focused on our opinions and ideas, sometimes at the expense of relationships. We can get carried away with defending our opinions at all costs. I've been guilty of fighting for my "right" thing to do and unwittingly making others feel bad in the process.

Author Bronnie Ware first wrote an online article based on her palliative care work that was later expanded in her memoir *Top Five Regrets of the Dying: A Life Transformed by the Dearly Departing*. The one theme she hears repeatedly is that relationships matter the most. Two of the five regrets are:

#2: I wish I hadn't worked so hard.

"This came from every male patient that I nursed. They missed their children's youth and their partner's companionship. Women also spoke of this regret. But as most were from an older generation, many of the female patients had not been breadwinners. All of the men I nursed deeply regretted spending so much of their lives on the treadmill of a work existence[2]."

#4: I wish I had stayed in touch with my friends.

"Many had become so caught up in their own lives that they had let golden friendships slip by over the years. There were many deep regrets about not giving friendships the time and effort that they deserved[3]."

From the many patients she's supported, Ware shares memorable, relatable stories of regret over too little time spent nurturing relationships. Using a different research methodology but arriving at the same theme, a Harvard University research project on adult development[4] tracked 724 participants over the course of seventy-five years to "identify the psychosocial predictors of healthy aging." The Harvard study found that the key to happy and healthy aging was strong relationships. Both the anecdotal palliative care work and the university research study emphasize investing in relationships.

Relationships involve building trust and empathy with the other person. They require slowing down to listen and understand where the other person is coming from. You don't need to agree with what they're saying, nor does their truth need to be yours. You don't have to pepper them with questions that might make them defensive. The first step is simply listening and validating the 10 percent of what they're saying that you can agree with. Mirror back 10 percent of what they're saying—you don't have to agree on anything else—and then build upon it using the "Yes, and…" technique from improv introduced in Chapter Two. Using this technique will continually make the other person feel heard.

As part of my own self-development into making space to change, I needed to consider the impact that I was having on other people. You see, I truly cared about people. My team was family. I was known for being fiercely protective of my team, like Katherine's mama-bear personality. To extend this strength, I experimented with reframing every single person I interacted with at work as "my team." This allowed me to be gentler with my judgements, both for them and myself.

I needed to drop my attachment to ideas. As a product person and designer, this was tough. The craft of a product designer is to come up with ideas and bring them to life in a prototype or video to paint this future vision for everyone else to see. Yet, ideas aren't the most important thing. Ideas are cheap. Many of the best ideas in Silicon Valley are copycats of other products and services. Good artists steal and adapt.

As I thought of the numerous products I'd launched through my career, I realized that I didn't feel the most pride about the products. Instead, I was most satisfied with the impact of the products on people's lives. But most of all, I remembered the people, the relationships, the culture, and camaraderie of getting to an idea together. People before ideas is the first principle for leading with intensity.

As Katherine worked with more teams and organizations, she couldn't solely rely on her brilliant ideas. That strategy had worked when she had built a trusting relationship with her first boss and when she'd brought along her handpicked team of intimates. As her responsibilities grew, she needed to make space and slow down to understand the different perspectives that her new teams had. She needed to listen to and acknowledge their fears over the latest re-org. She needed to first build the relationships and understand her people. Once that was in place, she could put forth a vision for the organization.

The first step is simply listening and validating the 10 percent of what they're saying that you can agree with.

CLIENT STORY:
EMBRACING HER QUIET LEADERSHIP

Jingyi ran a large product management team. She was a quiet leader, and despite having managed teams for years, she still had doubts as to whether she was good at managing people. She wanted to develop her own leadership style and effectively communicate upwards, particularly through advocacy with her boss and the CEO. It was important for her to find her own voice and use it in a style that felt authentic to her—collaborative and compassionate, not aggressive.

In our kickoff coaching session, we identified Jingyi's core values[5], the fundamental beliefs underlying what really matters to her. One value she identified was Solitude. To her, Solitude meant the ability to recharge and find her stability. It was a source of joy and energy. It provided mental space for her best leadership. Over the sessions, whenever Jingyi had to deal with a stressful presentation, we would return to her value of Solitude and make sure that she could build in enough rest time to replenish, both before and afterwards.

Jingyi was a fantastic champion for the people on her team. She was known for a uniquely collaborative workstyle of building consensus between aggressive naysayers early on in a project. Everyone knew that Jingyi could effortlessly diffuse tense situations; consequently, she was tapped to lead many of the company's biggest projects. Yet, she continued to receive feedback about needing to be "more vocal and visible" and that "assertiveness was a company value." This came to head after a leadership presentation that was described by her boss as "a shit show."

Jingyi was devastated and sure that she was going to be fired. First, we slowed down and processed some of the emotions and self-critical voices. We co-created some experiments for her to focus on each key relationship from her boss, to the CEO, to her peers. We changed the variables depending on the context and always played to her strengths. The different experiments included:

- Sending a detailed pre-read before meetings, taking the time to connect with her boss over non-work related topics
- Directly asking for ownership of certain passion projects

People before ideas is the first principle for leading with intensity.

· Building consensus around controversial topics before bringing them to the CEO

Over months, we built in time for her to slow down and reflect in solitude—on her calendar, she blocked time to walk her dog along the beach. Some of these experiments worked; others were failures. Yet, they were all ways in which Jingyi kept moving towards action on her career outcomes.

After several months of continuing experiments which built upon her quiet, collaborative leadership and her values, Jingyi gained confidence in her identity as a unique, quiet leader. She felt stronger as a writer than a verbal communicator, so she regularly sent pre-read documents before key presentations and follow-up emails afterwards. As she embraced what she had thought of as a weakness—her quiet tenacity and relationship-building—her reputation at the company grew. The feedback about needing to be "more vocal and visible" ceased.

Jingyi was known for being an understated, collaborative leader who got things done. Several months later, she got her coveted promotion to Vice President. But she was proudest of her internal shift: "I am comfortable with who I am as a leader. I am who I am, and I don't have to be like my boss or somebody else to be a successful leader. This is a much more comfortable state to be in."

FIND YOUR PEOPLE, FIND YOUR BRILLIANCE

I surf regularly with a group of people, many of whom paddle out daily, regardless of the conditions, while simultaneously holding full-time tech jobs. Every. Single. Day. I look at their dedication in awe as I only manage to get into the ocean once or twice or week. One of us obsessively maps out secret spots—a difficult endeavor in this crowded San Francisco Bay area coastline—and we'll go on adventures involving long hike-ins and—one time—rappelling down a cliff. When I'm in the water, I'm known for being a slightly reckless, aggressive surfer who goes for almost any wave, regardless of size or the proper positioning. Among the people I surf with, I'm the least skilled. I often end up wiping out and being held down in the water. The adrenaline gives me joy and it also makes me laugh. Unlike at work, I've always been okay with who I am in the water. I'm with this intense surf crew. These are my people.

Professionally, my insight moment about the difficult person story came when I observed the polarization: one cluster of people who never wanted to work with me again, and the larger cluster of people who followed me from company to company. The latter group was my people.

Katherine's people were the original team that she handpicked, and the hiring manager who saw her brilliance as the change agent to a slower paced enterprise software company. Being seen while interviewing allowed her to celebrate her intensity and her passion.

Jingyi's brilliance was turning her perceived weakness of being an introvert into a strength. She leveraged her collaborative, behind-the-scenes conversations to build consensus and became known as a quiet leader.

Imani was the brilliant engineer turned CEO from Chapter Two. She had a deep fear of judgement that interfered with her ability to openly promote her company and product. Her biggest strength was her depth of technical knowledge and her passion for solving complex problems. Her main leadership challenges were talking about the product and learning to ask for help from the many relationships she had in her network. These were closely connected and tied to her fear of being judged. As a first experiment, Imani focused on sharing the product with people she was most comfortable with—other engineers from her network. As her confidence grew, she made technical how-to videos to market the product. She leveraged her technical expertise to narrate the videos in a friendly human voice, a voice of the woman who also happens to be the CEO. These experiments leveraged her strengths in technical expertise.

Katherine, Jingyi, and Imani all learned to both find their people and find their brilliance. I learned to acknowledge my brilliance and to stop labelling myself as a difficult person. I am challenging and direct. I am unafraid of risks. I am highly emotional—I will dance with joy to celebrate your victory, and I will cry tears of empathy when touched by a story. I will push you to dream bigger and I will always speak my truth.

Find your brilliance by looking to your values, your strengths and your "weaknesses", such as Jingyi's introverted personality. Understand what you're known for and develop your leadership from those characteristics.

Unlike at work, I've always been okay with who I am in the water. I'm with this intense surf crew. These are my people.

To celebrate your weird and intensity, find your people. These are your champions who will lift you up and reflect your brilliance back to you. These are your superfans. You've built the relationships and trust with them, and they are one-hundred-percent onboard with your ideas and vision.

FOCUSING EXPERIMENT:
STRENGTHS AND WEAKNESSES

1. **What are you most known for?** List out your five biggest strengths and your five biggest weaknesses. They are often related as dual sides of the same coin. If you're at a loss, do some research. Think about four-six trusted people from different spheres of your life such as work, friendship circles and family. Ask them:

   • What do you think are my biggest strengths?

   • What are some things that I could do better?

2. **Pick one of your "weaknesses" and write down three perspectives around it, one negative and two positives.** The negative perspective is the one that you're most familiar with, and often expressed by your self-critic or your achievement monster. It's harder to write the positive perspectives. You could imagine what your best friend or biggest champion might project about your trait. If Jingyi were to do this exercise around her "weakness" of being quiet and introspective, she might write:

   Negative: I am too quiet at work. I need to be more assertive to express my opinions by being more vocal and visible in meetings.

   Positive: When I listen to others before speaking, it builds a collaborative atmosphere where everyone feels included.

   Positive: I am introspective and take time to form an opinion. This makes my writing stronger and more thoughtful.

3. **Focus and choose which of the perspectives you'd like to adopt.** Try it on for a couple of days and see if it makes a difference.

If this exercise resonates, you can repeat Steps #2 and #3 for all the traits on your list.

CHAPTER SEVEN

YEARNING FOR MORE

As we keep opening more space, we start to pay attention to the "should"s and the "must"s of our lives. We start to name them. In naming them, we can ask ourselves if the story is fact or fiction. One narrative that has run through my head for many years is that comparisons are bad. I **should** look to my own performance and not competitively compare myself to others. I **should** simply be me and not be so judgmental or jealous if someone else gets the impressive job, prestigious book deal, or gets barreled in a tube while surfing. We often beat ourselves up endlessly over these normal and very human feelings.

Comparing ourselves to other people is natural. We do it all the time, consciously and unconsciously. We learn this as children who seek to establish our identity amongst our peers, whether it's from the pressures of high-achieving parents or the desire to escape the home situation we're in. The first comparisons are with our siblings or cousins—who's prettier, funnier, smarter, or who do the adults love more. With our playmates, we analyze what we are given. *Did she get the most colorful marble? Did they get the biggest slice of cake? Why not me?* In primary school, we covet gold stars. We see how many we get and compare that to our friends. In later school, we see our class standing measured by grades given out on a curve. We look at who's picked first—or last—for playground games or sports teams. Comparisons are a way to measure how we belong and where our place is within a group of people. It helps us see ourselves in a certain way. We can find people who perform certain skills better than us and worse than us. Everyone explicitly knows how they match up to everyone else when picked for sports teams or being graded on a curve. We also implicitly know how we match up to everyone else. *She's funnier than I am. He's more attractive than me. I have more experience than he does. She's got better taste than anyone else. I'm better at drawing comics. He's more social.*

We apply to colleges that have an implicit quality ranking: from the Ivy Leagues, to renown schools for specific programs, to state schools, and to community colleges. There are tiers of companies to work for— world-class brand names or start-ups, international or local reach, and mission-driven or advertising-driven amongst others. Comparisons can be a source of motivation—they can help us desire and see examples of where we strive to be better. And they can affect us negatively when we look around and find ourselves lacking in contrast to our peers. *She got that promotion after only a year, and I've been waiting for two now. He bought a new Tesla Model X. They got pregnant so soon after marriage and we've been trying to conceive for years now. She got that C-suite job and now reports to the CEO.* It can drive us to self-judgement and wondering if we will ever get to that level.

Instead of focusing on envying others and listening to the voice of internal self-judgement, consider listening to the desire underneath the comparison. Ask yourself, what is driving that comparison? Perhaps it's an aspirational value we see in others, or an achievement we truly yearn for. Or perhaps it's ego-driven and we want it because someone else has it. Either is completely okay. Finding that kernel of self-knowledge within the desire helps us to grow and uncover our personal definition of success.

THE FACEBOOK PERFORMANCE REVIEW PROCESS

In my final year at Facebook, I was part of a small group that ran the performance review process for all the product designers working on the main Facebook app. We were responsible for making sure that hundreds of designers were evaluated equitably, given an accurate rating compared to their peers, and as related to the expectations of their job role and level. Most people got 'Meets All' or 'Exceeds Expectations'. On the higher end, you could receive 'Greatly Exceeds Expectations' or the very rare 'Redefines'. On the lower end, there was 'Meets Most' or 'Meets Some' which almost certainly led to a performance improvement plan being put in place for the employee. Every manager rated their own direct reports and then all the managers met in several hours-long sessions called calibrations to compare every product designer against each other. The purpose was to get to a stack rank[1] and to make sure that everyone who got a particular rating truly deserved it.

This calibration process is the master of all comparisons. And the rating really mattered—it determined bonuses, stock options, pay raises, and promotions. This performance review process caused huge anxiety for everyone involved. There was almost always disappointment. You might not get the rating you wanted; perhaps you got only a 'Meets All', or maybe you got a dreaded 'Meets Most' and you need to hustle to get your performance back on track. Or, it might be the coveted 'Greatly Exceeds' and you now have even more stress because you've reset your baseline— now you're terrified that you won't be able to keep achieving 'Greatly Exceeds' next half.

The most difficult thing with comparisons at Facebook, was that I was working with some of the most talented peers in the world. People have confided to me that it gets harder every year because everyone gets better and better. Being so transparently judged for your performance inevitably leads to imposter syndrome: feeling that you don't belong, that you lack the skills to do the job, and that no matter what rating you get, you're a failure.

Here's how to mitigate those feelings. When you look at the performance review process, keep in mind that performance reviews are solely for the company's benefit—not yours. Like grades in school, with a large enough company, there's a curve or an ideal distribution for how many people are in the top ten-percent, next ten-percent, average and so on. By definition, the majority of employees will be average and get a 'Meets All Expectations' rating. This feels difficult when it happens to us because we all like to believe that we are above average. But that's not how a company works. It's hard to feel that 'Meets All' is a good rating. For high achievers, who are used to having been the best throughout their lives, it feels mediocre, like getting a C in school. But if you're a top performer working in a competitive industry or a world-class company, the comparison pool is of the highest caliber. This system doesn't exist to help make you feel better about yourself, it exists for the benefit of the company to provide more products and get greater returns for shareholder value. Try to remember this at the time you need it most.

A different approach is to reframe the performance review as being selfishly for you and your growth. Look at comparisons as a source of learning. They can be a tool to give you insight into the areas you wish to improve and grow. Or, if you slow down and make space, you might learn that it's okay to NOT make the changes needed to reach a certain rating. Perhaps it's a day job and you have a side gig that's your passion. Perhaps you aren't willing to devote that much mental energy to your work. Perhaps you refuse to compromise on dinner time with your kids or choir practice with your performer family. You can slow down and make space to identify your own desires. Let's learn how.

CLIENT STORY:
FINDING DESIRE IN SLOWING DOWN

One of my clients, Isadora, had been driven by comparisons her entire life. She did well in school, in her first jobs, and quickly got promoted to the coveted position of managing teams. She worked at name-brand companies and continuously climbed the career ladder. She was always running fast and comparing herself to others. Isadora was driven by the external success metrics of achieving another raise, getting more people and projects on her team, and landing the next promotion. She never stopped to consider what felt good to her; she just kept going after the next rung on the ladder. When she saw other people getting recognized, she figured that she should also want those same achievements. The corporate system of success values climbing up the career ladder to get closer to the CEO level. To Isadora, success was measured in corporate terms: making more money, having a bigger team, a more important title. Those things are what garner respect in Silicon Valley. This was how she judged herself versus her peers.

There's nothing wrong with seeking external validation. It's useful feedback to let us know how we're doing and how other people see us. As humans, we all care about feedback. Yet there can be a danger in always judging ourselves according to external measures of success.

When COVID-19 hit last year, all of us had to slow down and adjust to a different way of living. In this period of ambiguity, something shifted for Isadora. Because the entire world went on pause, she didn't have to play this hyper-competitive game anymore. She could reclaim the fields of emotional and psychic energy that had been drained by her constant striving.

Non-essential working professionals had a collective break from the toil of career success and instead, could focus on surviving in this strange new world, while sheltering-in-place. The pandemic gave Isadora the opportunity to break an existing pattern and see what lay on the other side. For the first time in her life, she had freedom from continually striving, climbing, and comparing herself to others. She had the external permission to give herself time to slow down and think. She took time during 2020 to go inwards and think about what she really wanted.

As they were all confined in one house, Isadora spent more time with her partner and their three children. She saw the rhythms of success, joy, overwhelm, and frustration that everyone went through each day. She took the extra time to consider what gave her energy, what she truly enjoyed, and what her strengths were. From that place of reflection, she could take inspiration from what other people did—the comparisons—and chart her own career path.

By the end of the first pandemic year, Isadora had learned from her pause time. She left her current company and joined another whose leadership team aligned more with her values of integrity, collaboration, and support. She celebrated her personal strengths of being caring and compassionate. She understood her rare ability to lead teams with the supportive guidance of being a hands-on, but never micro-managing, boss. Rather than staying on the promotion track of her existing company, Isadora followed her yearning. She chose to make a lateral move that followed her values and gave her fulfillment.

HOW TO LEARN FROM COMPARISONS

Performance reviews are one of the toughest examples of comparisons. Rather than marinate in the envy, guilt, and negativity of comparing your shortcomings to others or worrying about how you might keep up this pace, recognize that these feelings are natural and put them to work for you. Start to open space by asking yourself research-oriented questions to find what an internal, intrinsic motivation might be.

1. WHAT CAN YOU LEARN?

Like Isadora, notice what triggers the envy you feel and the comparisons you make with other people. For many of us, the comparisons are around money, title, and prestige. These are the most easily accessible external markers of success. Dig deeper and consider all the facets around working with that title or level of responsibility. Think about the skills you want to learn or opportunities you can explore on the job. Try practicing these skills, in whatever small experiment is possible, and monitor how much you enjoy it.

Jonny was a product manager who was considering whether to switch to a more hands-on, craft-oriented role either as a designer or as an engineer. He wanted the freedom and cachet of doing the work himself instead of relying on others. Rather than leave his current job, I challenged him to have a conversation with the engineering director, which led to a plan for him to work with a mentor and be responsible for a small part of the code base. Jonny's small experiment in learning uncovered his next steps on the journey.

At larger companies, there's often the opportunity to show impact at the company level by contributing to initiatives such as recruiting, diversity and inclusion resource groups, or working with interns. You could find opportunities to share your expertise through teaching, speaking, or writing. Consider what you want to learn and get better at. Many designers will pick an area of craft to focus on for six months or a year. This could include learning to code, becoming a master prototyper, creating vision videos, or print-based graphic designs.

I was able to spend a lot of time at Facebook coaching women across the company, working on diversity efforts within the design organization, as well as broadening our pipeline to seek out more diverse interns and university hires. All these skills supported me later when I switched into leadership coaching. As you run these experiments, you can take external feedback to evaluate how the experiments are going. Are you good at these things? Do you like doing them? Do they give you energy?

2. WHAT IS GOING WELL?

In the midst of these comparisons, it's easy to focus on what you lack and what other people have. Take a moment to stop, and in the case of performance comparisons, ask yourself why you work at your current job. I've heard a variety of reasons including:

- It's a name-brand top-tier company/ Their clients are the top name brands
- I want to impact people's lives at scale
- I value the mission of the company
- It pays well and I need the money to finance other parts of my life
- I'm simply grateful to have a job that pays me and is the start of a career

These reasons may resonate, or you may have your own different reasons. Be clear with yourself about why you work there. Thinking about this will remind you that no job is perfect, and the next "dream job" will also have challenges. Reminding yourself of the reason why you joined, and focusing on what is going well, will get you through the long hours, the difficult feedback, the conflicts with other people—and remind you of the purpose of your professional life.

Many people know this when they apply for a job and decide to accept the job. We're excited for the shiny new opportunity and the ability to reinvent ourselves. Yet we forget after months or years and get taken over by the external success metrics of the culture. For example, telling ourselves "I'll be happy when..."

- ... I get that raise or bonus
- ... I get promoted to the next level
- ... I start managing managers
- ... I make partner
- ... I make it to the C-suite

I tend to be an impatient person and want to make change quickly. However, when I slow down to focus on learning, it helps me to reset my expectations of timeframes.

Yet, the goalposts keep moving. When we attain one promotion, we turn around the next day to plan how to achieve the next one. And this happens even more when we watch other people attaining those goals and feel the sting of negatively comparing ourselves to them. Instead of tying happiness to a future event, focus on what's happening where you are right now. Write down what went well today. Share your gratitude for something that happened today with a friend or partner. Acknowledge a specific small action that a team member took today.

3. WHAT'S THE TIMEFRAME?

Finally, when we compare ourselves with others, we only have a limited lens of where they are right now. We can't know how many late nights they've been working and for how long. We don't know their entire career journey and what sacrifices they've made to get to a particular point. We don't know their individual stories or what unconscious biases they had to overcome. Making space opens up curiosity. We can seek more information and understanding by reaching out to these people we're comparing ourselves to. We can learn more about their process, their sacrifices, their time frames, and their individual stories. More importantly, we can use these inputs to inform our own growth and learning. I tend to be an impatient person and want to make change quickly. However, when I slow down to focus on learning, it helps me to reset my expectations of timeframes. Clients tell me that it feels oh-so-important to get that desired promotion in the next six to twelve months. Waiting longer than that feels like an eternity. The fear sets in that we're not good enough because we know that our colleague managed to do it in less time. We set ourselves up to feel like we've failed by pre-determining an urgent timeframe that's based on nothing other than our own impatience.

Making space to focus on learning lightens the pressure of false urgency. Instead, focus on the desires and celebrate what is going well to get a better sense of the internal success that the comparing-to-others can help drive.

Comparing ourselves to others leads us to yearn for more. Instead, we can look inside ourselves and our unique leadership. Perhaps all the things that we thought were wrong with us could be strengths. Building our capacity for understanding allows us to be open to more possibilities.

Perhaps all the things that we thought were wrong with us could be strengths.

EXPERIMENT:
THE RITUAL OF CELEBRATION

Driven performers have gotten to their existing success because they practice continuous improvement to fix what's wrong. That only gets you so far. It can feel like acknowledging success can make us too soft or that we don't deserve to slow down and celebrate where we're at. This experiment is to shift perception to equally value what's going right—so we can do more of it—and not simply focus on what's wrong. It slows us down to appreciate our success.

1. **At the end of each day or each week, write down what you're proud of.** It could be a project accomplishment, a mistake you've made, or a relationship breakthrough with a troublesome employee or a peer. Dig deeper to explore why you're proud of each item. Bonus points: if you're feeling especially daring, share this list with someone else. It can be invaluable for a team to see this humility from their leader.

2. **Expand this ritual of celebration to include your team or company.** Either in a team meeting or asynchronously, try taking five-ten minutes to share what each person has been proud of that week or month. If this is a new ritual, you will likely have to be the first person to share. It can be helpful to ask a friendly team member to prepare to speak up.

CLIENT STORY:
FINDING MORE OUTSIDE YOUR CORE JOB

Chido (from Chapter Three) jumped from job to job with a restless spirit, searching for the next bit of excitement that might happen in a new environment. He found satisfaction when returning to a prior job where he was able to work remotely during the pandemic. We met Alexis in Chapter Four as she moved out of Silicon Valley to Texas seeking a reprieve from the pressure of climbing the corporate ladder. Alexis stayed in her existing job but felt freer to express her individual weirdness in the culture of "Keep Austin Weird." In the past, both

Chido and Alexis kept moving companies, continually chasing external success and comparing themselves to others.

That path wasn't sustainable, so they each tried something new. Rather than looking at the surface comparison of title and money, they went deeper in a brainstorm to explore what else might matter to them. They experimented to see if they could find that contentment while staying within their existing jobs as design leaders. I asked them to capture who they were jealous of and the deeper why behind the jealousy. As we brainstormed, they both had a common desire—to create their own personal leadership brand by giving back to the greater community of designers in some way.

For many people I work with, professional meaning outside of their job can come from:

- Individually mentoring more junior people in the field
- Teaching classes or workshops to share your lessons learned
- Speaking at conferences to share a case study, passion topic or a personal experience
- Writing or blogging to share your stories
- Creating a podcast or zine to promote a particular passion
- Starting your own creative projects outside of work, whether they're solely for yourself, pro bono, or freelance

All of these are choices available outside the core traditional role of working at a start-up or tech corporation. For his first baby step, Chido chose to start writing and individually mentoring junior designers. For her experiment, Alexis pitched her boss and got permission to teach workshops within her company. Depending on what she learns, the next step in her journey might be expanding workshops outside the company.

OPENING EXPERIMENT:
BRAINSTORM YOUR DESIRES

Use the energy of creativity to open up multiple possibilities. If we use the technique of brainstorming, it's about generating as many ideas as possible with no judgement on the quality of the idea. It's about quantity not quality. The more ludicrous the idea the better. Ideation gets out all the craziness, the humor, the absurd…and, somewhere within this vast quantity of ideas, there might be something that's worth trying. The rules of brainstorming are:

1. **Create as many ideas as possible.** I'm not talking about coming up with five ideas for getting unstuck, instead go for fifty or five-hundred.

2. **Build on the previous ideas.** You can use the "Yes, and…" technique from improv introduced in Chapter Two, to take one little part of an existing idea and expand it to go in a different direction.

3. **There are no wrong ideas.** The weirder and crazier the better. Being specific helps.

If we were to brainstorm where else professional meaning outside Chido or Alexis' job might come from, the list could include ideas that are both specific and silly such as:

- Become a yoga teacher
- Train the cat to use the toilet and share the process on Tik Tok
- Buy a wheel, build a kiln, and make your own pottery
- Crash a wedding and give a toast
- Write a short story of an aspiring designer trying to break into tech
- Enter a competition to build robots that serve tiki-inspired cocktails

- Make a satire short film or meme of the worst feedback from creative directors
- Go to circus school and learn to swing on the trapeze

If you get stuck, dive deeper into one of the items to find the kernel of what's important for you. From there, see if you can find other ideas that speak to the same kernel. For example:

I want to go to circus school because I've always wanted to perform.

I could try other performances. Perhaps I'll try out for The Moth to share my story.

Maybe I can add some storytelling to my team meetings. Will others want to share?

At the end of this process of brainstorming your desires, see if you can pick one small baby step to try to experiment with.

OPENING EXPERIMENT:
WHAT WOULD X DO?

Another opening experiment is to look at examples of people around you to discover your yearning.

1. **Think of leaders who you admire.** Capture their traits or values that you admire. Write down their accomplishments that you wish were yours.

   For example: *I admire Amanda Gorman for her resilience in overcoming a speech impediment and her classic yet distinctive fashion sense. I admire a poet, especially one that incorporates personal themes of oppression and race.*

2. **Think of people doing activities that fascinate you.** What is it about their story that tugs at something you might want?

   For example: *Penelope bought a 4x4, and in her 40s, is taking nine months to drive from Cairo to Cape Town. That feels so free and adventurous to me.*

3. **Finally, when you're looking at a work situation or decision, think, 'what would Amanda Gorman do?'** Or what would the adventurous option be? How might you incorporate aspects of this comparison and turn them into a small change in how you show up at work or in life?

Rather than listening to the "should"s and beating ourselves up when we negatively compare ourselves to others, instead find the core of what matters in the comparison. Make space to uncover insights for what you might be yearning for. Give yourself the permission to dream and yearn for more.

CHAPTER EIGHT

THE FLOW OF CREATIVITY

One key aspect of opening to space is understanding ease and flow. I believe that flow is tied to our innate creativity. What happens when you hear the term creativity? Does it make you nervous? Do you feel like you're not a creative person? It's okay, those feelings are normal. We're talking about flow and you don't have to be a designer, an artist, or self-define as a creative to feel flow.

We've all felt this at some moment in our life. That flow state, where you're so immersed in whatever you're doing that the hours fly by. Your energy is high, and the project feels effortless. For some people, it's baking for hours to perfect that sourdough loaf. For others, it's a piece of woodworking to craft a bookshelf or to whittle away at the block of solid wood until it reveals the beauty of a spoon inside. For others still, it's coding that elegant piece of problem-solving syntax or pulling together just the right widgets and components for a user interface screen. It feels so good to be in this flow state. To be in the creativity of making. Yet that feeling can be quite elusive. We want flow, but we are more likely to be stuck in a creative block, procrastinating with Netflix and social media until we're finally out of time and must force ourselves to painfully complete the chore at hand. The paradox is that the harder we try to force ourselves to complete the project, the more difficult it is to achieve the flow state. The path to creativity is one of ease and flow. We must learn to stop trying so hard and instead build the conditions for creative flow into our lives.

The paradox is that the harder we try to force ourselves to complete the project, the more difficult it is to achieve the flow state. The path to creativity is one of ease and flow.

TRYING TOO HARD FOR THE PERFECT CREATIVE SOLUTION

When I worked for design firms, we often had to be creative under time pressure. We estimated our work based on a set number of hours and knew that it would typically take a certain number of days or weeks to get to a solution. Understanding this process meant that we could give our clients a predictable sense of time frames and expectations of deliverables when working with us. I knew the set of structures and processes that would generate creativity and lead to solutions. Often this creativity happened naturally, in a flow state where the magic of an interdisciplinary team coming together would create a wonderful solution. But when it didn't, I became a taskmaster. I would never slip a schedule or let the client down. I only had one mode as a Do-er—never fail to meet a commitment. I was the hammer that had a single speed—go fast to grind it out—and I was determined the team would keep going to force creativity to happen. I couldn't simply let it be.

Now, of course, I realize that I was being ridiculous. I recognize that creativity is not something that can or should be forced. Instead, the most creative solutions, with their art and beauty, only come with the openness of space.

Fast forward some years to when I left Facebook to start my own business. Unlike the decade I spent at multiple design studios, this time I was the client. I was helping a coaching company, Positive Intelligence, create the next version of their coaching app to help people change their mindset by intercepting and shifting their saboteur voices. Their CEO, Shirzad Chamine, had helped me recognize my own Restless saboteur that continually sought distraction with shiny new objects. Part of my role was leading the re-branding effort for the company, and we had engaged a talented creative studio.

We had fantastic collaboration, working together for weeks leading up to the exciting moment when the first round of concepts was unveiled. Yet as the studio presented direction after direction, each of them felt wrong, like they were striving too hard to be something else. Our hearts sank. The creative studio had been trying too hard to force an identity resulting in a conventional quality to the design work. We asked them to go back to the drawing board. The day before our next meeting, we got a

Instead, the most creative solutions, with their art and beauty, only come with the openness of space.

note from the Creative Director at the design studio—they needed more time to get the feel of it right. My first reaction was irritation. The voice in my head said: *We're on a schedule. We must keep going to make sure we hit our dates.*

I realized that I was letting my self-critical, achievement monster drive me. Quite ironic given that we were building products to help people work with their saboteurs. Even more so when this brand was about finding your emotional intelligence and getting into flow. I made space to pause and focus on what really matters. Then it hit me: they were asking for much-needed space to find the right creative solution. The irritation relaxed, switching into trusting the process.

Two weeks later, we saw the next round of directions. They hadn't one-hundred-percent nailed it, but there was a new sense of freedom and ease in these concepts. The designs reflected the fluidity of the company and the flexibility of the coaching approach. The design studio had the confidence to stop the process and give themselves the freedom for creative exploration when ease and flow was missing.

I was deeply inspired. I had never been able to do this when I was the Creative Director. I would never have had the courage to pause the schedule and tell our clients that the work wasn't there yet. I would have kept soldiering on, forcing it and pushing it through.

"SLOWING DOWN IS SOMETIMES THE BEST WAY TO SPEED UP."

—MIKE VANCE, DEAN OF CREATIVE THINKING

It's not possible to force creativity to a schedule or a previously determined destination. Like the creative studio, sometimes you need to hit reset and slow down. Hiccups and mistakes in the creative process are inevitable. Focus on the process, not the outcome, to best optimize yourself for the state of flow.

EXPERIMENT:
SLOW DOWN TO SPEED UP

When we're stuck and find it difficult to see our way out of a problem, one misguided but common way forward is to try harder. I've frequently fallen into this trap. We forcefully argue our point. We keep researching ways to continue our current path. We find data to uncover new paths. We bear down and work harder. Instead, consider slowing down to speed up.

- If you're working on a solo problem, take a break and shift your energy. You could call a friend for a chat, take an intentional break to browse social media for ten minutes, pet your cat, or move your body with a walk outside or some other exercise.

- If you're working with a group, stop and name what's going on. You can use a phrase like:

  "It feels like we're all trying too hard. Can we take a moment to pause?"

- Next, ask the group to consider a different approach. Some options include using questions like:

  ○ "What would this feel like if it were easy?"

  ○ "How might we shift the energy to enjoy reaching this goal together?"

  ○ "What really matters to us here?"

Finally, schedule permitting, take a break and resume after some hours or overnight.

THE FLOW OF SURFING

In the spring of 2021, I met up with a dear friend in Santa Cruz to surf. We hadn't spent much time together since the start of the pandemic, and he'd been focused on raising a new baby boy. It was Super Bowl Sunday and not many people were out in the water. The waves were uncharacteristically small that day, which was especially rare—the Northern California winter tends to have massive, ten-foot plus waves. I switched out my usual shortboard and borrowed a longboard from my friend. Shortboards are useful to fight your way out to the lineup and duck-dive underneath the breaking waves. I prefer riding a shortboard. It allows for a late risky take off and once I'm up and riding, it feels quick and powerful. In contrast, with more surface area, longboards take a slow and effortless approach to catching waves. It can be a longer, more intentional paddle followed by an unhurried dance down the line of a wave. We bobbed together in the water, my friend and I, basking in the warm California sunshine. Any wave was catchable, so we lazily paddled for the little bumps and had long, pleasant, knee-high rides all the way to shore. In between, we kept up the conversation: caught up about our kids and partners, how we'd handled the pandemic, and updated each other on our mutual passion for personal growth.

"Are you paddling out every day now?" he asked me. He assumed that once I left Facebook and was making my own hours, that I'd be surfing every day and spending even more time with my daughters. He had a good memory—these were both reasons I'd cited for leaving the corporate world.

"Actually," I replied sheepishly, "I've been too busy to surf. I make it out in the water maybe every two or three weeks." I rattled off excuse after excuse, sharing all the things I was doing. *Clients in Europe taking up the prime early morning surf time. All the new programs I was launching. The speaking engagements. This book I was writing.*

Both the gentleness of his curiosity and the slowing down to enjoy longboarding made me realize that even though I had left Facebook to escape the cult of busyness and to take a step back from my corporate achievements, I couldn't escape my inherent need to keep on grinding and filling my non-parenting hours with working. The irony sank in—I had the freedom to run my own business yet felt indebted to working hard all the time to make said business successful.

That insight led me to try an experiment. I committed to getting in the water two or three times a week, prioritizing the space of surfing in my life. It only took a week for me to clearly see the results. I noticed that when I started out a day in the water, my work was better. I had high energy, my mood was more positive, and any creative output—from writing to teaching to creating programs—was of magnitudes better quality. Slowing down to surf clearly got me in better creative flow.

The irony sank in—I had the freedom to run my own business yet felt indebted to working hard all the time to make said business successful.

Surfing is about finding the right space. It's picking the right break to paddle out into, a combination of wind, tides, and the wave energy in the ocean that creates a swell. It's about selecting the right board for your ability and the conditions. This is the structure and work that goes into creating a flow state. In the water, flow comes from taking stroke after stroke in a persistent rhythm. Flow comes from sitting on the board bobbing up and down with the ocean energy. And finally, flow comes from positioning yourself in the right space to take off and catch a wave, dancing your way with the board along the edge of a wide-open face of the wave.

CLIENT STORY: BEING ENOUGH

When the pandemic hit, Isadora (from Chapter Seven) was able to slow down and let herself take a pause from the constant comparisons and climbing up the career ladder. She ultimately decided to make a lateral move to a new company that hit all the work facets that mattered for her—culture, leadership, people, including former colleagues she would reunite with, and mission.

For the first time in her professional career, Isadora took a month off between jobs. She approached her new position fresh and excited about the dream job. When we spoke, she was six weeks into the new job and completely overwhelmed.

"I've been on a running speed train for the last six weeks. I've been exhausted every single day. There's simply too much on my plate."

As we spoke, she realized that she had reverted to her patterns. Her habits followed her to this new job—she needed to be hands-on, to control the direction of her team, and instantly provide value.

I reminded her of her word for the year–"enough." As we looked to what she wanted for 2021, she had picked that word to ground herself and return to her state of flow. She shared the yearning behind the word: "Internally I need to feel enough. To be in flow in the present rather than chasing new things." *Enough* brought her back to knowing that she was a talented leader who had proven herself many times over. Her leadership team trusted her from their prior relationship at different jobs. She was skilled at building relationships with her cross-functional peers and was known to be a leader with high quality standards and huge compassion for her team members.

With this gentle reminder of her word, Isadora was able to pause and slow down for herself. She focused on what mattered—building stronger relationships with her team, her managers, and her peers. She felt her energy grow and she built connections. She was in a flow state as she nurtured her allies, and built her identity as a caring, compassionate leader. Isadora stopped doing constantly. Instead, she was enough.

MAKE SPACE FOR S.U.R.F.

As we wrap up these stories of ease and flow, I'm leaving you with a reminder on how to integrate all the experiments from this book to take baby steps every day. Make space for S.U.R.F by:

S – Stop to notice what's happening. Be aware of old patterns.

U – Understand what truly matters. Start with your yearning.

R – Re-. Pick your own *re-* word. Re-create, re-think, re-imagine, re-do. Whatever opens you up to new perspectives.

F – Force and Flow. Which one do you want more of today? The structures of force or the flow of creativity?

S. STOP TO NOTICE WHAT'S HAPPENING

I've interviewed hundreds of designers while at Facebook. Every incredible designer and leader I've worked with—no exceptions!—has had a single common trait, self-awareness. We all make mistakes, we're only human. The beauty of self-awareness is to understand what we're great at and what patterns we'd like to change. Being self-aware helps us to stop ourselves, take a pause and notice what's happening. Start to notice:

- The emotion that you feel, especially if it's a negative one such as anger, resentment, or fear. Notice how strongly you feel the emotion.

Isadora stopped doing constantly. Instead, she was enough.

- How your body is reacting. Your body can provide a first subconscious warning sign before your brain has the chance to catch up and think about the situation. Look at places of common tension in the body such as your jaw, throat or shoulders. Feel what's happening in your chest or your gut. Notice your breathing and your heart rate. Is it elevated or calm?

- Your energy level right now. Are you open and vibrating with others? Are you buzzing with intensity, whether from excitement or fear? Are you drained and ready to be done? Are you hungry or tired?

- Are you repeating an old pattern? Has this followed you from job to job or relationship to relationship?

Name what is happening. Say it out loud to yourself or to a confidante. Try to let go of judgement or self-criticism. Simply stop and observe what's happening.

U. UNDERSTAND WHAT TRULY MATTERS TO YOU

Next, put on your researcher hat and get curious about what's happening. This is where you can use a combination of your powerful thinking brain and your intuitive gut. When in the process of understanding, recognize if you've seen this pattern before. It might be familiar with a similar story or recurring players. Remember to understand from a place of strength not a place of fear. Yes, fears and achievement monsters also exist but the stories they're telling you might not be true.

Remember:

- Be curious and compassionate.
- Understand with your head and your gut.
- Look for patterns.
- Try to uncover your strengths in this situation.
- Name your fears, whether it's an achievement monster or another story that's holding you back.

For more tools, go back to the research inquiries at the end of Chapters One through Three or reference the Wheel of Leadership from Chapter Four.

R. RE-

My achievement monster wants me to find the perfect word for R. In contrast, the rebel part of me wants to question all acronyms and offer up alternatives for the different letters. Honoring both parts, I invite you to pick your own Re- word that resonates with you. Re- is about doing something again or anew. Sometimes it's looking backwards to help see the way forward. Sometimes it's a transition to an opposite state. Consider these re- words:

- Re-create
- Re-think
- Re-ignite
- Re-imagine
- Re-do
- Re-bel

Pick your own Re- word. After you've stopped and tried to understand, next figure out what you want to do differently. Use your Re- word to open yourself up to new possibilities and perspectives. Create the next experiment that's right for now.

F. FORCE AND FLOW

Finally, even in this chapter on creative flow, the F stands for both force and flow. We've talked a lot about flow. In both design and leadership, I've witnessed flow come from following a process of opening up to new perspectives and then choosing some narrower actions to focus on. Underlying this design process is the patience to wait and trust that the ideas will come, and they will land when least expected.

Have you ever had the experience of going to sleep wrestling with a thorny problem and then, after a night of restful sleep, you wake up seeing the brilliant solution?

What about having a moment of inspiration in the shower or while taking a walk through the park?

On the other side of the equation is force. This happens when we build in the conditions for creative flow by establishing structure and routines. We create actions and experiments to move us forward. Creating the structure is the force. For example, we can use our calendar to build in focus blocks (from Chapter One) each week. We can set our phone or wearable device to remind us to take a stretch break every couple of hours. Beyond a calendar, we can establish habits to get away from behind the computer screen and into real-world activities that generate flow, such as: cooking, baking, woodworking, or painting. We can create intentional structures to spend time out in nature, such as hiking or taking a walk in the woods.

Many clients who first start working with me need force. Structures include:

1. The rhythm of working with a coach on a regular basis to establish a long-term goal.

2. Identification of what experiments to try next.

3. Creating an action plan based on the experiment results and the accountability of an external partner to help hold them to it.

Establishing these structures of force ensure that flow can happen. Both force and flow are needed in the design process and to make more space in our lives. Contextually, in the S.U.R.F model, you decide for each situation whether you want to add a bit more force or add a bit more flow. Each decision will have aspects of both.

KEEP MAKING SPACE

The S.U.R.F. model is meant to be a reminder of how to keep making space in our lives. Being in flow gives us permission to let go and not continually push forward. It requires both the structure and the patience to take the long view. It requires integrating the data and facts around the issue or problem you're working with and letting your intuition continue to process while you're not actively focused on it. It honors the Be-ing part of you, not just the Do-er.

Trust that divergence—opening to multiple perspectives—and convergence—focusing on a choice or action—will work.

Trust the process.

I'll keep pushing and sharing this message of making space to leaders in and out of the technology world. We all need to make space for what matters. I continually need to remind myself of this as I push myself to grow my business, scale my impact, and build a movement for the world to make space to lead. And, I will slow down when I unplug and relish being in nature.

The beauty is that there's always another chance. Another day. Another wave. Even in my busiest times, I've always intuitively known to find my best self out in the water. I wish that peace for you as well.

Bye for now. I'm going surfing.

ACKNOWLEDGEMENTS

I'm grateful to all the people who made *Make Space to Lead* possible, starting with the clients I've supported. I've been inspired by each one of you and your voices are represented in the composite client stories throughout the book.

As an ambitious and clueless first-time author, I'm thankful for all the guides on this speed-train of a book journey through 2021. Thank you, Sarah Chauncey, for seeing my complexity. You held space for my impatience and my drive, and always encouraged more surfing. Thanks, Jim Herman, for the laughs, the multiple detailed readings and always on-point feedback. With gratitude to Dino Marino, the most talented book designer, always willing to patiently collaborate with my detailed "suggestions." Thanks to Patti M Hall, my first reader and book coach, Wendy Muruli and Shamaila Anjum of Tessera Editorial for your meticulous copyediting and proofreading, and Marie Incontrera for the creative promotion.

WITH DEEPEST GRATITUDE:

To the coaches and personal guides who have encouraged me towards more introspection: Karen Ericksson, David Darst, Rich Litvin, Shirzad Chamine, Rosy Elliott, Nicholette Routhier, and Kendra Cunov.

To the writers and teachers who inspired my thinking: Jennifer Aaker & Naomi Bagdonas, Tara Brach, Steve Chandler, Dorie Clark, The Conscious Leadership Group, Bruce Feiler, Jane Friedman, Gay Hendricks, Alana Karen, Patrick Lencioni, Wallace J. Nichols, Andy Polaine, Leonard Szymczak, Chris Voss, Bronnie Ware, David Whyte, and Julie Zhou.

To my co-leaders over the past two years. Maria, you showed us how to improvise like jazz musicians. Jim, you've annoyed me into letting go and being more playful. Irene, I'm so grateful that all aspects of our relationship—from college roomies to co-teachers—have been equally effortless and full of love.

To my invaluable community: The CTI Qwirkle pod, the Project Kairos Dream Team, Donna Lichaw who made me feel not alone, and to Deborah, Ted, and Nicole who kept my sanity with our Fab Four weekly check-ins.

To my SF surf crew. Charlie for inspiring my return to the water and creating this community: Eric, Brad, Allan, Spencer, Enrique, Nico, Casey, Rafael, Lily, Aaron, Jeff. Thank you, Ryan for Lemoore.

Unconditional love and gratitude to my family: Sariya, Anisa, Mochii, and Boba. Josh, I appreciate this journey we continue on together.

To Sister. Love you always, even if you didn't read the first draft. To Moe and Irene, for your bountiful love and support through these hard years of change.

To Toben. We've experienced these precious years of transition together. You've seen and supported me like no one has ever done before. Together, we learned how to love deeply. The photos and Mr. Eaves are a bonus!

TO MY FRIENDS, FAMILY, CLIENTS, AND LAUNCH SUPPORTERS:

Adam D, Adam W, Ahsia B, Allati E H, Allison P, Amara T, Anastasia F, Andres J, Ashwin N, Betsy B, Bob R, Brad D, Cara D, Charlie G, Chris F, Christina B, Courtney K, Danielle R, David T-K, Desi B, Divya S, Elijah S, Erin B, Gertraud E, Gilad K, Helen Z, Holly K, Ina L, Irene S, Ivy L, Jen R, Joan K, Kelli C, Key L, Kimberly A, Laura B, Marisa R, Milo H, Misha C, Narisa T, Natalie S, Natasha M, Paula G, Pouneh M, Ravit B, Richard DLR, Rino M, Rod T, Rosanna L-M, Sandra W, Sarah F, Sauragh G, Shermaine M, Shivani G, Sophia H, Sreedhar R, Susan L, Tory H, Uday G, Vero J, Vidhu S, Wei Z, Xiaochen Y, Xuan W.

NOTES

CHAPTER ONE: OVERWHELMED BY BUSYNESS

1 Abraham Joshua Heschel, "Moral Grandeur and Spiritual Audacity: Essays"

2 Kevin P. Madore, Ph.D. and Anthony D. Wagner, Ph.D., "Multicosts of Multitasking," April 1, 2019, https://www.ncbi.nlm.nih.gov/pmc/articles/PMC7075496/

3 Gijsbert Stoet, Daryl B O'Connor, Mark Conner & Keith R Laws, "Are women better than men at multi-tasking?," October 24, 2013, https://bmcpsychology.biomedcentral.com/articles/10.1186/2050-7283-1-18

CHAPTER TWO: THE FEAR OF NOT ACHIEVING

1 Reid Hoffman, "If There Aren't Any Typos In This Essay, We Launched Too Late!" March 29, 2017, https://www.linkedin.com/pulse/arent-any-typos-essay-we-launched-too-late-reid-hoffman/

2 Andy Polaine, "Escaping your personal escape room," January 9, 2021, https://www.polaine.com/2021/01/escaping-your-personal-escape-room/

CHAPTER THREE: DISTRACTED BY SHINY OBJECTS

1 Shirzad Chamine, company and website. https://www.positiveintelligence.com/

2 Shirzad Chamine, Saboteur Assessment description of the Restless saboteur, https://www.positiveintelligence.com/assessments/

3 The Enneagram Institute, The Enthusiast Enneagram Type Seven https://www.enneagraminstitute.com/type-7

CHAPTER FOUR: THE DISCOMFORT OF NOT KNOWING

1 Brené Brown, Unlocking Us podcast, "Brené on FFTs",
March 20, 2020, https://brenebrown.com/podcast/brene-on-ffts/

2 Coactive Training Institute website, https://coactive.com/

CHAPTER FIVE: BREAKING OLD PATTERNS

1 Coactive Training Institute coach training program https://coactive.com/

CHAPTER SIX: UNDERSTANDING YOUR INTENSITY

1 Edward De Bono, "The Six Thinking Hats"
https://www.debonogroup.com/services/core-programs/six-thinking-hats/

2 Bronnie Ware blog, "Regrets of the Dying,"
https://bronnieware.com/blog/regrets-of-the-dying/

3 Ibid

4 Harvard Second Generation Study, Grant & Glueck Study,
https://www.adultdevelopmentstudy.org/grantandglueckstudy

5 Tutti Taygerly, "The Value of Values," July 17, 2020,
https://www.tuttitaygerly.com/blog/the-value-of-values

CHAPTER SEVEN: YEARNING FOR MORE

1 Wikipedia article, "Vitality Curve,"
https://en.wikipedia.org/wiki/Vitality_curve

ABOUT TUTTI TAYGERLY

Most people know Tutti as a design leader with twenty-two years of experience building products and design cultures in the world's largest organizations. Today, she's an executive leadership coach to entrepreneurs and technology leaders who make a real impact in the world.

Tutti has led teams at startups, design agencies, and large tech companies. Most recently she spent four years at Facebook creating video and advertising products. She's run design at a Series B funded startup, opened new offices as General Manager for a development consultancy, and been the Creative Director leading vision for clients including Google Fiber, Microsoft phone interfaces, Sony entertainment, and Samsung devices. She's also crafted digital experiences to extend the magic of Disney beyond the parks and resorts.

Tutti has spoken at multiple conferences including the Lean Startup and South by Southwest. She has written for *Business Insider* and *Fast Company*. Tutti is a certified coach through the Co-Active Training Institute and has a B.S. in Human-Computer Interaction from Stanford University.

What most people don't know is that while Tutti appeared to be successful, her drive came from continually seeking external validation—moving from valedictorian to Stanford and then effortlessly up the corporate career ladder. She kept working longer hours to launch innovative products and better support her teams, yet it became harder to feel the creative flow and the meaning in the work. She discovered the power of coaching as a wake-up call and it also became her path to entrepreneurship.

Tutti has been an insatiable adventurer and risk-taker her entire life. She grew up in seven countries on three continents and is settled in San Francisco as her home base. Tutti spends her time parenting two spirited girls, obsessively reading, and paddling out for the next wave.

Find her at www.tuttitaygerly.com.

EXPERIMENT WORKBOOK

To continue the conversation, download your free copy of the *Make Space to Lead* Experiment Workbook. It includes all the experiments from this book in an easy-to-print format so you can start running your own experiments.

Download it for free at

tuttitaygerly.com/makespaceexperiment

COLOPHON

This book was set in Garamond.

Mr Eaves XL Mod OT was used in the cover title and interior chapter titles.

Rockwell slab was used for the cover subtitle and interior chapter numbers.

The book cover has corduroy waves inspired by photos from Ocean Beach. The foremost breaking wave is from a personal photo taken at Trestles in Southern California

Mr Eaves XL was designed by Zuzana Licko from Emigre fonts. It's a derivative of Mrs Eaves, named for John Baskerville's (designer of the Baskerville typeface) wife Sarah Eaves.

The author adores the feminism and meta-ness of the naming.

Cover and Interior Design: Dino Marino

Made in the USA
Las Vegas, NV
09 November 2022

59075630R00092